James Fallows

POSTCARDS FROM TOMORROW SQUARE

JAMES FALLOWS is *The Atlantic Monthly*'s national correspondent, who has been based in China since 2006. He is a former editor of *U.S. News & World Report* and a former chief White House speechwriter for Jimmy Carter. His previous books include *Blind Into Baghdad: America's War in Iraq*; *Breaking the News: How the Media Undermine American Democracy*; *Free Flight*; *Looking at the Sun*; *More Like Us*; and *National Defense*, which won the American Book Award for nonfiction. He has been a finalist for the National Magazine Award four times, and his article about the consequences of victory in Iraq, "The Fifty-first State?" won that award in 2003.

ALSO BY JAMES FALLOWS

Blind Into Baghdad: America's War in Iraq

Free Flight: Inventing the Future of Travel

*Breaking the News: How the Media
Undermine American Democracy*

*Looking at the Sun: The Rise of the New East Asian
Economic and Political System*

More Like Us: Making America Great Again

National Defense

*Inside the System: The Five Branches of
American Government* (with Charles Peters)

Who Runs Congress? (with Mark Green and David Zwick)

The Water Lords

POSTCARDS FROM TOMORROW SQUARE

POSTCARDS FROM TOMORROW SQUARE

REPORTS FROM CHINA

James Fallows

VINTAGE BOOKS

A Division of Random House, Inc.

New York

A VINTAGE BOOKS ORIGINAL, JANUARY 2009

Copyright © 2009 by James Fallows

These articles in this collection were previously published in
The Atlantic Monthly:
"Postcards from Tomorrow Square" (December 2006)
"Mr. Zhang Builds His Dream Town" (March 2007)
"Win in China!" (April 2007)
"China Makes, the World Takes" (July 2007)
"Macau's Big Gamble" (September 2007)
"The View from There" (November 2007)
"The $1.4 Trillion Question" (January 2008)
" 'The Connection Has Been Reset' " (March 2008)
"China's Silver Lining" (June 2008)
"How the West Was Wired" (October 2008)
"Their Own Worst Enemy" (November 2008)

Library of Congress Cataloging-in-Publication Data
Fallows, James M.
Postcards from Tomorrow Square: reports from China / by James Fallows.
p. cm.
"The articles in this collection were previously published in The Atlantic Monthly."
ISBN 978-0-307-45624-3
1. China. 2. China—Relations—United States. 3. United States—Relations—China. I. Title. II. Title: Reports from China.
DS706.F3 2009
951.06—dc22
2008028083

Author photograph © Deborah Fallows
Book design by R. Bull

www.vintagebooks.com

Printed in the United States of America
10   9   8   7   6   5   4   3   2

For Deb

CONTENTS

INTRODUCTION

The chapters in this book were written between the summers of 2006 and 2008, when my wife and I were living first in Shanghai and then Beijing and were traveling through many other parts of China.

This was not our first experience in the country. We had visited China in the mid-1980s, when we were living in Malaysia and Japan with our elementary-school-aged children. Getting into China was tricky at the time. We had finagled a visa by studying the invented language Esperanto, as a family, so we could be part of the U.S. delegation to the 1986 World Esperanto Congress in Beijing. (A friend was head of the U.S. Esperanto League.) There we spoke with Chinese intellectuals who had been assigned to learn Esperanto rather than English at the height of anti-Western sentiment under Chairman Mao.

The country then was still dark, poor, and monochromatic. Big city streets had few lighted signs or storefronts at night. Wardrobes were drab blue or gray. The idea of China becoming an economic and financial powerhouse seemed highly speculative.

In Shanghai we met a Chinese man in his late seventies who seemed eager to use his British-accented English, dormant for decades, in conversation with us. During Shanghai's racy and European-controlled era in the 1930s, before the Imperial Japanese army arrived, he had been a clerk in the Shanghai office of a London-based brokerage house. He showed us a brittle stock certificate from that era, which he had hidden through all those years, and said that he hoped to live to see the Shanghai Stock Exchange reopen. Five years later, it did open. I never learned whether his hope was fulfilled.

After this first exposure, I visited China again on reporting trips in the late 1980s and 1990s. Then, after several years of planning, in 2006 my wife and I moved from our home in Washington, D.C., to Shanghai and other cities for three years or so. It has been just over two years now as I write this introduction. For me this meant writing a series of articles for *The Atlantic Monthly*, for which I had also been a correspondent during our previous time in Asia. My wife continued her work for a U.S.-based Internet research firm, studying the Internet's evolution and effects in China.

Most of the material that follows appeared month by month in *The Atlantic*, starting late in 2006. It is presented here in its original sequence, as an unfolding report on China's changes during this period—as it solidified its role as a dominant manufacturing and financial influence on the world as a whole; as it coped with increasing domestic and foreign criticism about its environmental problems; and as its press, people, and government prepared for the Olympics and responded to a series of crises prior to their start. These included a freak snowstorm that paralyzed travel in the southern half of the country, just as tens of millions of people were joining their families for the Chinese New Year holidays; international protests and disruptions as the Olympic torch relay passed through; and of course the devastating Sichuan province earthquake on May 12, 2008, which killed perhaps 100,000 people and left many millions homeless.

Naturally, the sequence of articles also reveals the changes in my own attitudes and conclusions over these two years. And they illustrate the two different approaches I have taken in trying to explain what I have seen.

Some of the articles collected here deal with questions that I had in mind before coming to China. But many of the articles are about people, trends, and events that I had not known were interesting or significant until I came across them after we had arrived. This opportunity for discovery is the real payoff of life as a reporter: the chance to answer questions you did not previously know you wanted to ask.

For instance, until I happened to visit his hometown of Changsha, in Hunan province, I had never heard of Zhang Yue, the entrepreneur described in the second chapter of this book. On the home campus of his air-conditioning company in Changsha, Mr. Zhang has built a replica of the Palace of Versailles plus a 130-foot high golden-colored pyramid. He also operates one of China's first corporate air fleets—and meanwhile reveres Al Gore for his attempts to deal with climate change. I ended up thinking not just that he was intriguing in his own right but also that his story would give outside readers some sense of the wild variety of personalities, interests, and visions among the new business class in China.

Similarly, I had not known about the dominant role of reality shows on China's state-run TV networks until I had a chance to watch some of them. When I did, I became fascinated by the drama and the implications of a show called *Win in China!* that was modeled on Donald Trump's *The Apprentice* but was more earnestly pro-entrepreneurial in its approach. It is described in chapter three. The same process of unintended discovery led me to the story of how two Taiwanese-born business executives undertook the mission of reducing poverty in China's dry, remote western provinces, as portrayed in chapter ten, and of the Irish-born entrepreneur Liam Casey's emergence as "Mr. China" in the southern manufacturing center of Shenzhen, described in chapter four.

Here is the main thing I hope readers will bear in mind in considering the variety of these chapters—short or long, "policy"-oriented or devoted mainly to portraying interesting cultural developments: The most important fact about them is, indeed, the *variety* of the aspects of China they present.

I suspected before coming to China, and now know for sure, that no one can sensibly try to present the "real story" or the "overall picture" of this country. It is simply too big and too contradictory.

The point may seem obvious, but I emphasize it because I believe that many people who lack firsthand experience in China have not fully taken it to heart. A central problem in the way the outside world thinks and talks about China is that it assumes there is a single, comprehensible "China" to discuss.

Every country varies; the challenge of China is that its internal variations are truly enormous. Given China's scale, they are probably greater than those of any other country. They are certainly greater than what outside politicians and citizens usually assume in discussions about China's economic and strategic potential and their own future dealings with it. Yes, press and politicians in other countries routinely refer to the huge and widening gap between China's haves and have-nots. But that is only one of countless important cleavages within the country—by region, by generation, by level of schooling, by rural versus urban perspective, even by level of rainfall, which determines how many people a given area of land can support. The situation of entrepreneurs in Guangdong province, north of Hong Kong, has almost nothing in common with that of subsistence farmers in Sichuan or Hebei provinces. People who lived through the Cultural Revolution have a different sense of how perilous "rapid change" can be for China than do their children, who have known only the current boom. The millions of Chinese people who have returned after living abroad have a different sense of their country's situation than the billion plus who have never left. And on through a very long list of other differences.

All of these are intensified by a factor evident to most people on the scene but omitted from much outside discussion: the tremendous individualism and nonconformism of Chinese culture. In this sense, the spectacular opening ceremonies of the Beijing Olympics, which featured huge regimented masses (most of them soldiers detailed for the task) performing in perfect synchronization, may in the long run prove damaging to China's cause. They increased the impression that the country is one big supercoordinated hive; as I hope this book conveys, the reality is much the reverse.

Why does this matter? I think that even now the Western world's limited familiarity with China, especially its under-appreciation of the cleavages within the country, leads to two important problems: an overestimation of China's power and a misestimation of its strengths, weaknesses, and possibilities.

A clear sign of overestimation is unrealistic bullishness about where China is heading—and its converse, unrealistic fear about what its rise might mean for everyone else. Both assume that the people and systems in charge of China's development are more foolproof and farsighted than they could possibly be. The impression of perfect control over all things at all times was another of the implied messages of the Olympic ceremonies, but it matches very few of the daily realities that I have seen and that I describe in this book. In chapter six, "The View from There," I quote Susan Shirk, of the University of California, San Diego, who in 2006 published a book on China called *China: Fragile Superpower*. The writer Frank Gibney had used the same term thirty years earlier in a book about Japan; it seemed even more apt for China, given its much greater scale. But Shirk said that when she discussed the book with Americans, they always asked, "What do you mean, *fragile*?" When she discussed it with Chinese, they always asked, "What do you mean, *super-power*?"

Behind that difference, as she explained, was a Chinese awareness of countless obstacles to the economy's continued rapid growth: pollution, social unrest, commodity and water shortages, pricing itself out of the cheap-labor manufacturing market, and others discussed in the chapters that follow. It often seems that managing China's growth through the last quarter century has been like steering a boat down treacherous white-water rapids. So far, the people in charge have managed to avoid each boulder just before crashing into it—but there's always another boulder looming. That the Chinese leaders have dodged so many boulders so far is impressive; how many more they'll avoid, no one knows.

Overestimating China is a particular political and psychological risk for the United States. If Americans believe that China's rise is "unstoppable," perhaps they will respond in ways that do themselves and their system credit: shoring up the weak parts of their own educational and economic system, trying to become the best possible versions of themselves. This was the best aspect of the "Sputnik crisis" of the late 1950s, when the Soviet Union seemed to have attained an unreachable lead in science and technology. But anyone who knows American politics understands the risk that Americans will respond by indulging a lesser version of themselves, becoming more impatient, closed, and accusatory. At worst, this could involve casting China as something that, in my view, it need never become: a military threat to the United States.

Whether or not outsiders overestimate China's strength,

they are very likely to misestimate it, which in turn can lead to blunders even if they do not consider China a threat or rival. The contention that outsiders need to stop and understand what they are really dealing with in China explains the contrarian tone of several chapters that address politics and policy. When researching "China Makes, the World Takes," I started looking for evidence of how, exactly, China's emergence as the factory of the world affected the places where factories used to be. The evidence I found convinced me that—so far—it had helped China and Chinese people without hurting *overall* most other countries, though some people in those countries have clearly been forced out of traditional markets, businesses, and jobs. China's continued dominance of manufacturing could create new problems, for reasons I examine in this chapter; but I argue that to cope with those when they appear, or even to understand where and why they might pose dangers, people outside China need to think clearly about the positives and negatives of what has happened so far.

Something similar is true of "The $1.4 Trillion Question," which if adjusted for exchange rates and China's ever-mounting assets would be more like "The $2 Trillion Question" as I write. During the 2008 U.S. presidential election, candidates from both parties depicted this as yet more evidence of the Chinese threat. I contend that it certainly reflects an imbalance in the financial structure of both countries, and that it is not good for either in the long run. But the effects of the imbalance are, for now, much worse on China. The money being loaned to and invested in America is money that

China's own people, still on average very poor, cannot use to build the schools and sewer systems and smokestack-scrubbers their own country needs.

"'The Connection Has Been Reset,'" chapter eight, explains why China's scheme for controlling the Internet is both less intrusive and more effective than most outside discussion assumes. It is surprisingly porous and flexible and allows escape routes for people who are really bothered by its limits—and who might protest more vigorously if they were entirely cut off from outside information flow. But the Chinese government's "Great Firewall" makes it just enough of a nuisance for ordinary Internet users to reach unauthorized Web sites that most of them don't bother. Instead they stay safely within controlled terrain. This has important implications for the way outsiders understand censorship in China and the way it shapes internal Chinese debate.. Finally, "China's Silver Lining" argues that the environmental predicament is as bad as outsiders assume—but also much better, since so many parts of China's political, business, and civic structure are now trying to cope with it. This understanding affects the way outsiders deal with China on future pollution and climate-change issues, since it suggests ways that China can be part of the solution rather than a huge problem.

These policy-oriented chapters, like the reports on some people and institutions of contemporary China, do not presume to be complete or final accounts. They offer a few parts of the complicated picture of China today. I hope they entertain and inform readers. But if they do no more than remind people of how complex the picture is, they'll have accomplished something.

A few practical notes: When my wife and I arrived in China in mid-2006, one U.S. dollar was worth eight Chinese yuan renminbi, abbreviated here as RMB; two years later, the dollar was worth about 6.8 RMB. In some places, where useful for clarify, dollar-RMB figures have been adjusted to reflect that change. Otherwise, the material has been left as originally published.

The Atlantic Monthly has been my professional home for more than twenty-five years. To recognize my colleagues properly would require listing every name on the masthead. I do thank past and present members of the *Atlantic* staff as a whole, especially James Bennet, Ben Bradley, David Bradley, Janice Cane, Ben Carlson, Abby Cutler, Marge duMond, John Galloway, Jennie Rothenberg Gritz, Terrence Henry, Teddy Kahn, Julie Klavens, Corby Kummer, Sue Parilla, Ellie Smith, Justin Smith, Sage Stossel, Scott Stossel, Maria Streshinsky, Jason Treat, and Jenny Woodson. For their generosity and help in China, and in the United States while we were in China, I would like to thank Phil Baker, Dominic Barton, Daniel Bell, Robin Bordie and Andy Rothman, Lila Buckley, Liam Casey, Dovar Chen, Peter Claeys, Melanie and Eliot Cutler, Jessica Dong, Patty and Marvin Fabrikant, Frank Fahrenkopf, John Flower and Pamela Leonard, Becky Frankel, Jeremy Goldkorn, Stephen Green, Dan Guttmann, Catharine Han, Susan Harrington and Alan Zabel, Andrew Houghton, Jiang Mianheng, Ken Jarrett, Kent Kedl, Kai-fu Lee, Kenny Lin, Kitty Leung, Yumin Liang, Andrew Lih and Mei Fong,

Adam Minter, Andy Moravcsik and Anne-Marie Slaugher, Russell Leigh Moses, Rebecca Nicolson and Tom Baldwin, John Northen, Minxin Pei, Lucia Pierce, Shaun Raviv, Sidney Rittenberg, Bob Schapiro, Baifang and Orville Schell, Shi Hongshen, Susan Shirk, Sherry Smith and Marcus Corley, Sun Zhe and Nina Ni, Tu Weiming, Jim and Bonnie Wallman, Sean Wang, Louis Woo, Jenny and Bill Wright, Jarrett Wrisley, and Zeezee Zhang. As always I would like to thank my literary agent, Wendy Weil; plus my editors, Dan Frank of Pantheon and Keith Goldsmith of Vintage.

This book is dedicated to my wife, Deb. We recklessly signed on as members of a volunteer work group in West Africa for our "honeymoon" just after we were married many years ago, and have been supporting each other in similar adventures ever since.

Beijing
September 2008

POSTCARDS FROM TOMORROW SQUARE

POSTCARDS FROM TOMORROW SQUARE

DECEMBER 2006

Twenty years ago, my wife and I moved with our two young sons to Tokyo. We expected to be there for three or four months. We ended up staying in Japan and Malaysia for nearly four years. We traveled frequently in China, Indonesia, Thailand, South Korea, and the Philippines, and we dodged visa rules to get into Burma and Vietnam. One year our children attended Japanese public school, which helped and hurt them in ways we're still hearing about. After our family moved back to Washington, I spent most of another year on reporting trips in Asia.

Not long ago [July 2006], my wife and I moved to Shanghai for an indefinite stay. You can't do the same thing twice, and we know that this experience will be different. Our children are twenty years older and on their own. We are, well, twenty years older. The last time, everything we saw in Japan and China was new to us. This time, we're looking at Shanghai to compare its skyscrapers and luxury-goods shopping malls with the tile-roofed shop houses and run-down bungalows we first saw here in 1986. The whole experience of

3

expatriation has changed because of the Internet, which allows you to listen to radio programs via Webcast and talk daily with friends and family via Skype.

But it still means something to be away from the people you know and the scenes and texture of daily home-front life: the newspapers, the movies, the range of products in the stores. (Most of America's ubiquitous "Made in China" merchandise is hard to find in China itself, since it's generally destined straight for export.) And the overall exercise is similar in this way: The Japan of the 1980s was getting a lot of the world's attention; today's China is getting even more. My family and I saw Japan on the way up. During the first few months we were there, the dollar lost one-third of its value against the yen. On each trip to the money-changing office the teller's look seemed to become more pitying, and on each trip to the grocery store (forget about restaurants!) we ratcheted our buying targets another notch downward. The headlines trumpeted the yen's strength and the resulting astronomical valuation of Japan's land, companies, and holdings as signs of the nation's preeminence. The dollar's collapse made us acutely aware of the social bargain that affected everyone in Japan: high domestic prices that penalized consumers, rewarded producers, and subsidized the export success of big Japanese firms.

China has kept the value of its currency artificially low (as Japan did until 1985, just before we got there), and because it's generally so much poorer than Japan, the daily surprise is how inexpensive, rather than expensive, the basics of life can be. Starbucks coffee shops are widespread and wildly popular in big cities, even though the prices are equivalent to their U.S. levels. But for the same 24 yuan, or just over $3, that a young Shanghai office worker pays for a latte, a construction worker could feed himself for a day or two from the noodle shop likely to be found around the corner from Starbucks. Pizza Hut is also very popular, and is in the "fine dining" category. My wife and I walked into one on a Wednesday evening and were turned away because we hadn't made reservations. Taco Bell Grande is similarly popular and prestigious; the waiters wear enormous joke-like sombreros that would probably lead to lawsuits from the National Council of La Raza if worn in stateside Taco Bells. Kentucky Fried Chicken is less fancy but is a runaway success in China, as it is in most of Asia.

Through my own experiment in the economics of staple foods, I have been surprised to learn that there is such a thing as beer that is too cheap, at least for my taste. On each of my first few days on scene, I kept discovering an acceptable brand of beer that cost half as much as the beer I'd had the previous day. It was the Shanghai version of Zeno's paradox: The beer became steadily cheaper yet never quite became free. I had an early surprise discovery of imported Sam Adams, for 12 yuan, or $1.50 per 355-ml bottle, which is the regular U.S. size. The next day, I found a bottle of locally brewed Tiger, the national beer of Singapore, for 7 yuan, or 84 cents per 350 ml. Soon I moved to 600-ml "extra value" bottles of Tiger at 6 yuan (72 cents per 600 ml), then Tsingtao at 3.90 yuan (45 cents per 600 ml), then Suntory at 2.90 yuan (35 cents per 600 ml). It was when I hit the watery, sickly sweet Suntory that I knew I'd gone too far. There was one step farther I hesitated to take: a local product called REEB (ha ha!), which I often saw the illegal migrant construction workers swilling, and which was on sale for 2.75 yuan. One night, in a reckless mood, I decided to give REEB a try. It was weaker than the Suntory—but actually better, because it wasn't as sweet.

The signs of China's rise are of course apparent everywhere. We can still see many parts of Shanghai that have escaped the building boom of the last two decades—the streets lined with plane trees in the old French Concession district, the men who lounge outside in pajamas or just boxer shorts when the weather is hot. But to see them we have to look past everything that's new, and the latest set of construction cranes or arc-welding teams working through the night to finish yet more projects. From a room in the futuristic Tomorrow Square (!) building where we have been staying, I can look across People's Square to see three huge public video screens that run commercials and music videos seemingly nonstop. The largest screen, nearly two miles away, is the entire side of the thirty-seven-story Aurora building in Pudong, Shanghai's new financial district. In the daytime, the sides of the building are a shiny gold reflective color. At night, they show commercials to much of the town. "People under thirty can't remember anything but a boom," a European banker who has come to Shanghai to expand a credit-card business told me. "It's been fifteen years of double-digit annual expansion. No one anywhere has seen anything like that before."

My family arrived in Japan just at the beginning of what is widely considered to be its collapse. About the strange nature of that "decline"—one that left Japan richer, and its manufacturing and trading position stronger, than it was during its "boom"—there will be more to say in later reports. But obviously it raises the question: Is this ahead for China? Have we arrived in time to watch another bubble burst? I don't know—no one can—but as a benchmark for later reports, I will mention some of the things that have surprised me in my first few weeks, and I'll do so via lists.

Numbered lists are popular everywhere—the Ten Commandments, the Four Freedoms—but they seem particularly attractive in this part of the world. When I first arrived in Japan, everyone was talking about the "Three Ks"—the three kinds of work for which the country was quietly tolerating immigrant labor. These were what translated as the "Three Ds": the jobs considered too *kitanai* (dirty), *kiken* (dangerous), or *kitsui* (difficult) to attract native-born workers in modern, rich Japan. During World War II, Japanese forces were notorious for applying a policy of "Three Alls" to occupied China: kill all, burn all, loot all. Memories of that slogan made for hard feelings when a Japanese-owned firm recently tried to register the trademark "Three Alls" (*sanguang*) in China; because of protests, the application was turned down. In early 2006 the Chinese government put out a widely publicized list of "Eight Honors and Eight Dishonors," or more prosaically "Eight Dos and Don'ts," to express what President Hu Jintao called the "socialist concept of honor and disgrace." For instance: Do strive arduously; don't wallow in luxury. I bought a poster with the full list at the local Xinhua bookstore.

In a similar constructive spirit, I now offer "Four Cautions and Two Mysteries." These are meant to illustrate what has surprised me so far and what I am most curious about. It is also a partial and preliminary agenda for future inquiry.

CAUTION ONE:
WATCH OUT, JAPANESE PEOPLE!

To get into a talk with a Japanese intellectual or statesman is sooner or later to ponder the effects of World War II. When will Japan emerge from the war's shadow as a "normal" nation, with a constitution written by its own people (versus the one created by Douglas MacArthur) and with a bona fide army, as opposed to something that has to call itself the "Self-Defense Force"? When will the Chinese and Koreans—and for that matter the Singaporeans and Filipinos and Australians—stop mau-mauing Japan with their wartime complaints? What special mission and message does Japan have for the world, as the first and only country to have suffered a nuclear attack? Will Japan's view of America always be skewed into an inferiority/superiority complex because of the U.S. role as conqueror in the war? The process is similar to discussions in Germany—except that Germans tend to be preemptively apologetic about the problems their forebears caused the world, and Germans make no special claim to suffering like Japan's.

The process is not at all similar to discussions about the

war on this side of the Sea of Japan. I put this item first, because for me it has been the most startling. "Frankly, we hate the Japanese," an undergraduate at a prestigious Chinese university told me in English. The main difference between his comment and what I heard from countless other young people was the word *frankly*.

Why should this be surprising, given the centuries of tension between China and Japan? Mainly because of the people who expressed their hostility in the most vehement form: students in their teens and early twenties. They had not been born, nor had their parents (nor even, in many cases, their grandparents), when Japanese troops seized Manchuria in the 1930s, bombed and occupied Shanghai, and slaughtered hundreds of thousands of Chinese civilians during the Rape of Nanjing. Wartime memories die hard, but you expect them to be most intense among actual participants or victims, and therefore to fade over time. Israeli teenagers aren't obsessed with today's Germans. I was not able to spend much time at universities talking with students when I was in China in the 1980s, but I don't remember anything comparable to today's level of bile.

The breadth of hostility surprised me for another reason. For years I have been skeptical of the idea of an anti-Japanese resurgence in China, viewing it as government-manufactured sentiment designed to deflect potential protest toward external enemies and away from the Chinese regime. In a new book called *China: Fragile Superpower*, Susan Shirk of the University of California at San Diego gives a detailed account of occasions when the Chinese government has deliberately drummed up anti-Japanese sentiment—or damped it down when it seemed to be getting inconveniently robust.

In a country where media and education are as carefully controlled as they are in China, all public opinion is to an extent manufactured. "The students are excited," a professor at a leading Chinese university told me. "They can be calmed down." Still, I don't view anti-Japanese sentiments as a ploy anymore. "You say anything at all about Japan [on a blog or computer bulletin board], and there will be ten thousand posts immediately," an official of a Chinese high-tech firm told me. "The mob effect can get out of control."

Partisans of Baidu, the main local search-engine company (which is listed on NASDAQ and has Americans as its main investors) recently ran a blog campaign touting it over Google. One illustration was Google's supposed inability to return any results for searches on "Nanjing Massacre" (or "Nanking," the older Western spelling), whereas Baidu returned plenty. There was a technical reason—Google's servers are outside China and thus must cross the government's "Great Firewall" to send results to users in China. The firewall routinely screens out references to "massacre," as in "Tiananmen Square massacre," and so it blocked Google's results. Baidu's servers and resources are all inside the firewall, and have been pre-scrubbed to remove references to Tiananmen and other prohibited topics. Google has since made adjustments so that it too can report on Nanjing, but the episode showed the sensitivity of the issue.

The main trigger for renewed Chinese protest against Japan has been the (idiotic) persistence of Junichiro Koizumi,

Japan's former prime minister, in paying ceremonial visits to Yasukuni Shrine, in Tokyo, where 14 Class-A war criminals from World War II are among the 2.5 million Japanese war dead the shrine honors. Koizumi recently stepped down after five years in office, but his successor, Shinzo Abe, has refused to rule out continuing the visits. When I've asked Chinese students what they want from Japan, they often say an end to the Yasukuni visits and "an apology." Formal apologies have in fact been offered many times by Japanese officials, and even by the current emperor. If the Chinese are looking for something like German-style ongoing contrition, this is not in the cards. Twentieth-century history, as taught in Japan, holds that Japan itself was the ultimate victim of the "Great Pacific War," because of Hiroshima and Nagasaki.

There is one tantalizing further twist to the syndrome. When I have asked young people why they should be so wrapped up with events seventy years in the past, the reply is some variant of: "We Chinese are students of history." There are certain phrases you hear so often that you know they can't be true, at least not at face value. Yes, China's years of subjugation by Western countries and Japan obviously still matter. But the history that is more recent but less often discussed is that of the Cultural Revolution, from 1966 to 1976, when the parents of today's college students were sent into the countryside and often forced to denounce their own parents. In an eloquent new book called *Chinese Lessons*, John Pomfret of *The Washington Post* recounts the ways that his classmates from Nanjing University, where he was an exchange student in the early 1980s, bore the emotional and even moral imprint of

11

those years. They'd been made to do things they knew were wrong, and they found ways to rationalize away that knowledge. So far every student gathering I've been to has included a volunteered reference to the evil Japanese, and none has included a reference to the evils of Chairman Mao (whose picture is still on every denomination of paper money) and his Cultural Revolution.

CAUTION TWO:
WATCH OUT, OLYMPIANS!

If you've ever doubted the impact of big international spectacles, consider the examples of Beijing and Shanghai. Beijing will of course host the Olympic Games in less than two years; Shanghai will have a World's Fair in 2010. In Japan, I often heard that the 1964 Olympics represented a turning point in world opinion. I saw a similar effect in South Korea during preparations for its 1988 Olympic Games. In the mid-1980s a countdown clock in Seoul's main square showed the number of days until the Olympic opening ceremony. The clock was a dramatic sight during the antigovernment protests of 1987, when the number of days remaining was barely visible through drifting tear gas.

I've seen countdown clocks in Beijing, Shanghai, and Qingdao, the coastal city that gave its name (with a different English spelling) to Tsingtao Beer and where the Olympic sailing events will be held. China certainly seems to be taking the spectacles as a major turning point. Posters with morale-building slogans are everywhere—and the English versions that appear beneath the Chinese characters are often touching. (This is the place to say: While trying hard, I still have no working command of spoken Chinese and rely on interpreters. I can generally read posters or newspaper headlines because of similarities with written Japanese.) "If the world gives us a chance, we will return it many splendors," reads the English line of an Olympic poster in Shanghai. The English on Qingdao's poster reads, "Civilized Qingdao Greeting the Olympic Games."

The construction and refurbishing under way for the Olympics and the World's Fair are phenomenal. Shanghai has five functioning subway lines now—and functioning very well, with better features than I have seen on any public-transportation system anywhere in America. (Plasma screens in all stations show the seconds until the next train's arrival; an advanced E-ZPass–style fare system lets you pay with one card for subways, buses, taxis, and ferries; LCD screens in the subway cars show entertaining short advertising videos; there is cell-phone coverage in the subways and just about everywhere in Chinese cities; etc.) The city is supposed to have *thirteen* lines by 2010. During several days in Beijing, I found it hard to look anywhere without seeing a road, sewer, stadium, or hotel being built.

Many aspects of the new, improved China will be up for the world's inspection during the Olympic Games. But there is one little catch: the air. Unless something radical changes, I do not understand how athletic events can take place in air as dirty as Beijing's. I am not a sissy: I grew up outside Los Angeles and have been to Mexico City, Bangkok, and other environmental hellholes. During the first few weeks my wife and I were in Shanghai, we wondered whether the pollution talk was all a big scare, since the skies were beautiful and blue. Then the typhoons that had been freshening the airflow over China (and drowning thousands of people in the southern provinces) petered out, and Shanghai developed a serious haze. But I've never, even in the worst ozone-alert days of my youth, seen anything like Beijing.

There are reasons for its problems—Beijing, like Los Angeles, sits in a sunbaked basin that traps pools of air. There are also solutions. Big industrial plants are being moved out of town, and everyone assumes that when the time comes for the Games, the authorities will do whatever they have to—closing factories, banning private traffic—to bring pollution down to an endurable level. On my first drive into the city from its Capital Airport, in the summer of 1986, I saw pathetic little rows of saplings. Now impressive stands of trees line that same route. Throughout the city, gardens and green spots have been created, and they appear to survive. *Still.* If the marathon runners, or even the archers, can finish their events without clutching their chests and keeling over, the Chinese authorities will have accomplished something special.

CAUTION THREE:
WATCH OUT, AMERICA!

One thing I have learned through travel is that every country is unhappy with its school system. The reasons for unhappiness in America are familiar. In Japan, China, and South Korea, the complaint is that memorization for national university admissions exams creates a generation of unimaginative zombies who are so overstressed by the time they reach college that they sleep, shop, or play video games through the next four years. "America is heaven until you are eighteen," a Chinese professor said, using a slogan I later heard from others. "China is hell." Despite a memorization-and-exam system as onerous as any country's, South Korea is enjoying a vogue right now as a source of creativity. Its cartoons, its televised soap operas, its clothing fashions, even its Samsung mobile phones are popular in both China and Japan. South Korea's recent pizzazz, however it has been achieved, has only intensified long-standing and often-voiced dismay in China and Japan over how to make their students not just technically competent but also "imaginative" and "creative." The distress is particularly acute in China, because, contrary to what most Americans would assume, the Chinese government spends so little on education, and so much of what it spends is concentrated on a handful of elite schools. Overall, China spends just over 3 percent of its gross domestic product on education at all levels, about half as much as the average for developed countries. "Most of the money goes to the top ten schools, and what goes to the top ten mainly goes to the top few," a professor at one of the favored schools told me. This makes getting into the "best" name-brand schools—like Tsinghua and Peking universities in Beijing, and Fudan and Jiao Tong in Shanghai—all the more important, which in turn increases the need for students to cram for tests and the advantage for those who go to high-fee private high schools.

I think I've seen the answer to China's education problem—and in a way, to America's. It is to make sure that young Chinese people keep coming to the United States—some for college, and very large numbers for graduate school and for work.

It is possible to feel an abstract generational envy—oops, I mean a vicarious excitement—for educated Chinese in their teens through their early thirties. They know that their country is on the rise, and while its political problems are enormous, their prospects are brighter than those of any previous generation in the long history of their culture.

Within this favored group there is a smaller set that seems particularly fortunate. These are the native-born Chinese who have spent a few years studying or working in the United States. An American software entrepreneur I met here (when he was visiting his company's subsidiary in Hangzhou) explained his theory that modern economies and cultures are driven by "tribes" of people on the move. The tribe of Jewish scientists and intellectuals who fled Hitler transformed America's intellectual life after World War II; the tribe of graduates from the Indian Institutes of Technology is heavily represented in Silicon Valley and has greatly contributed to innovation and enterprise there. Young Americans who served overseas during World War II or in the peace corps in the 1960s had a lasting effect on America's relations with the world—and the hordes of young Mandarin-speaking Americans I keep bumping into in China could do the same.

The tribe of "returnee Chinese" seems very important to today's China. My impression may be skewed, since I have met so many of these people at universities and in technology or financial companies. But I think anyone would find them, on average, a formidable group. From growing up in China, they learned (apart from the language) how to operate in this culture. From being in the United States, many of them learned (apart from the language) traits still very difficult to cultivate in China itself. These include professional managerial skills; the idea of open academic debate, even with one's elders; techniques for funding start-up firms and other organizational structures that encourage innovation; and a sense that bribery, petty or grand-scale, is at least in principle wrong.

And most of them seem to have liked the process. The African students who trooped to Moscow and Beijing in the 1960s and 1970s often returned grumbling about mistreatment and racism; Americans who spend time in Japan often come away with love-hate feelings because of that culture's exclusiveness. Chinese returnees, based on all available evidence, are at least subconsciously pro-American. They have made friends and followed sports teams; many have raised culturally Americanized children. Despite obvious differences of culture and language, and despite obvious exceptions to the rule I am about to propound, on the whole Chinese people get along with Americans, and vice versa. Because returnees have usually been part of either a university or a company in the United States, when they come back to China they're more likely to think of working with General

Motors (a huge success here and the leading automaker, with the locally manufactured Buick its most prestigious brand) or UCLA than with the counterparts from Japan or Europe.

If I were China's economic czar, I would recycle as many of the country's dollar holdings as possible on grad-school fees in the United States. And if I were America's immigration czar, I would issue visas to Chinese applicants as fast as I could, recognizing that they will create more jobs, opportunities, and friends for America than the United States could produce any other way for such modest cost. Many Americans will nod along with this point in principle. I would have, too, a few weeks ago. I'm saying that I feel it viscerally now, having met some of these people and begun to see their role in China. And to hear them say that their younger counterparts are going instead to Australia, England, or even Japan because of U.S. visa restrictions makes me want to say: America, wake up and watch out!

CAUTION FOUR:
WATCH OUT, EVERYONE!

It is too bad that "land of contrasts" is such a cliché, for there are situations in which it would be handy. Trying to make sense of the combination of rigid control and the near-complete chaos the newcomer sees in China is one of those.

I don't mean to sound flip, because one side of this contrast, the regime's repression and authoritarian controls, is a grave matter. Apart from its effect within China, it is likely to be the main source of friction between the United States and China for years to come. Every day's paper since I've come to Shanghai, and every hour's set of blogs, has brought news of some fresh assertion of state control. An internationally famous activist named Chen Guangcheng, blind since childhood, was convicted on charges of "organizing a mob to obstruct traffic" after he protested official misconduct. (Famous elsewhere, but not in China; I have found that few university students recognize his name, since Chinese media did not highlight his case.) Ching Cheong, a reporter from Hong Kong, was sentenced to five years in prison on apparently trumped-up charges of espionage.

Until I installed a "proxy server," which allows my computer to tunnel under and around the "Great Firewall," I was amazed at the parts of the Internet I could not reach from China. Technorati.com, for no obvious reason. Wikipedia. Both sites were mysteriously unblocked in October, but then I had trouble with Google News. One URL I can always reach is the central government's very useful official Web site, www.gov.cn, which has an English page. Naturally it highlights the upbeat: A white paper on "China's Peaceful Development Road" has as its first chapter, "Peaceful Development Is the Inevitable Way for China's Modernization." But, to its credit, it also includes announcements of the latest restrictions on commerce, banking, and the news media.

A list of the tensions between individual rights and the interests of the state could be very long. On the other hand, at least on brief exposure, urban China hardly feels like a hypercontrolled or overpoliced society. You can arrive at the Beijing or Shanghai airport thirty-five minutes before a scheduled domestic flight without needing to break into a nervous sweat. Few police are in evidence at the airport, and the security lines are short. (This is not because air travel is such a rarefied, elite taste in China. Fares are relatively low, and the China Eastern Airlines shuttle flight I took from Shanghai to Beijing was a 747 with all seats filled.) Every instant of life in East Germany under the Communists or in Burma under its ruling generals reminded you that Big Brother was in control. Walking down Shanghai's main shopping boulevards, Huaihai and Nanjing roads, makes you think you are in one vast bazaar. You can hardly walk a block in Shanghai without passing a vendor selling pirated DVDs for less than $1 apiece. Viewing these has given me my first inklings of sympathy for the Motion Picture Association of America: I never have to spend much for a movie in China, but the versions of movies I can see are terrible. I missed *The Da Vinci Code* in America and bought a copy here. The dialogue had been dubbed into Chinese and then subtitled back into English—sort of. When Tom Hanks is told that descendants of Jesus and Mary Magdalene might still be alive, he asks incredulously, "BE? They on the hoof?"

I have not before been anyplace that seemed simultaneously so controlled and so out of control. The control is from on high—and for most people in the cities, most of the time, it's not something they bump into. What's out of control is everything else.

Often this is in a good way. On an evening walk down a

side street that looked little changed since the 1930s, my wife and I started noticing that nearly every person we passed was running a business of some sort. This man was riding a bicycle with a towering load of flattened-out cardboard, meant for a scrap dealer. That old woman was weaving together rice straws for a broom, helped by her toddler granddaughter who handed her straws. A middle-aged woman sat outside her house working on a sewing machine. A vendor who looked as if he had just trudged in from the countryside tottered along with a heavy yoke across his shoulders, balancing two heavy baskets full of peaches. Another man was selling crickets in tiny individual straw cages. It makes you marvel at Mao's delusion in thinking that China could be a centrally planned economy rather than a beehive of commerce.

One reason why Americans typically find China less "foreign" than Japan is that in Japan the social controls are internalized, through years of training in one's proper role in a group, whereas China seems like a bunch of individuals who behave themselves only when they think they might get caught. As I took an airport bus from downtown Tokyo to the distant Narita International Airport for the trip to Shanghai, the squadron of luggage handlers who had loaded the bus lined up, bowed in unison, and chanted safe-travel wishes to the bus as it departed. When I arrived in Shanghai, I saw teenage airport baggage handlers playfully slapping one another and then being told by the foreman to get back to work. In Japan, the controls are built in; in China, they appear to be bolted on.

A less attractive side of China's social bargain comes in public encounters. Life on the sidewalk or subway may have been what Thomas Hobbes had in mind with his "war of every man against every man." As technology, Shanghai's subway is marvelous; as sociology, it makes you despair. Every person getting on a subway understands that there will be more room if people inside can get off. Yet the more crowded the station, the more certain that there will be a line-of-scrimmage standoff as the people trying to surge in block those trying to escape. In a perverse way, I was relieved when I read that China's traffic-death rate per mile driven was nearly ten times as high as America's: I wasn't crazy in thinking that the streets were a reckless free-for-all. The writer Gwynne Dyer recently explained that such carnage is typical of cultures in which virtually everyone behind a wheel is a "first-generation driver," raised with no exposure to traffic laws, defensive driving, or the damage cars can do. As more Chinese travel abroad as tourists, and China prepares to welcome more foreign travelers when the Olympics begin, the government has launched a "mind your manners" campaign urging people to stop "hawking" (noisily clearing their throats) and spitting on the street, to stop cutting to the front of lines, and to stop yelling at one another and into their mobile phones. Good luck!

The climate is that of the frontier, with an erratically vigilant sheriff showing up from time to time to crack heads. The untamed energies of individual Chinese have obviously helped the country grow, but some people have argued to me that the lack of Japanese-style collective virtues imposes limits on China. "We have a huge economy," the founder of a Chinese software company told me at dinner one night, "but we don't have any big companies. Why is that?" Depending on how it's measured, China's economy is either the third-, fourth-, or fifth-largest in the world. But only three mainland Chinese companies are among the top 500 in *Forbes*'s list of international companies, with the largest, PetroChina, at No. 57.

This man's answer was that scale requires trust, and "there is no trust in China." People don't trust others outside their family, he said. "They don't trust the Internet. Or doctors. Or the mobile-phone company to bill them honestly. Or, of course, the government." Building a company beyond the family scale requires many layers of trust: in accountants, underwriters, the financial markets, the rule of law. "People are all looking for the profit in the next two years, so they cannot grow," this man concluded. Would his company list shares on the stock exchange? "Ha!" he said. "The economy keeps growing, and the stock market keeps falling." The big problem for the markets is what financiers call "lack of transparency"—that is, the difficulty in knowing whether a given firm is making or losing money, and the suspicion that it is keeping several sets of books.

"Corruption, corruption, corruption!" another technology executive exclaimed to me. "You could knock off a hundred corrupt officials a day and you would not make a dent." To take just one indicative example: High government officials have recently found it desirable to be "scholarly." Thus universities have become accustomed to dignitaries who attend a few classes and soon get a Ph.D. Japan has always had its scandals—I was living there when police found gold bars and $50 million in the home and offices of Shin Kanemaru, a backstairs power in the ruling party. The most famous South Korean CEOs of the 1980s ended up in jail. But those countries—unlike Russia, the Philippines, or Indonesia—manage to keep their corruption within the "efficient" range, where it will not impede the growth of business. So far, China's corruption must also have been kept efficient—how else could the country have come so far so fast? But I've been surprised to hear how often corruption is mentioned as a major long-term threat.

And now we confront Two Great Mysteries of China, which concern its leadership and its ideals. I'm not referring to a host of Minor Mysteries I hope to comprehend over time. For instance, the miracle of the malls: how so much of Shanghai's showy new retail malls can be occupied by Prada, Armani, or Louis Vuitton stores—the real ones, not counterfeits—when there appear never, ever to be any customers inside. Who pays the rent? Or the miracle of the loaves: every run-down neighborhood has a bakery selling very good croissants and baguettes (though it is very hard to find cheese in China, which after all has no dairy-food tradition, and where a standard knock against Westerners is that they "smell like butter"). I am after bigger game.

Of course, it can seem preposterous for a newcomer even to raise such points, as if a foreigner in America observed that the country "is divided along party lines" and "has racial problems." But here are two of the many themes I want to know more about.

THE FIRST GREAT MYSTERY OF CHINA:
HOW SKILLFUL IS THE LEADERSHIP?

Everyone wants to know how long the Chinese economic boom can go on. Will an environmental crisis stop it? What about the gap between rich and poor? And between big shots on the take and peasants kicked off their land? After all, a nearly unbelievable 87,000 "public order disturbances" took place in China in 2005, according to China's own Ministry of Public Security, up from an already alarming 58,000 in 2003. What about the contradiction between a rollicking market system and an intrusive, controlling, one-party state? And what about a hundred other concerns amply documented in studies from China and around the world?

These are all ways of asking: Can China continue to adapt? In adaptability, Chinese society as a whole puts the rest of the world to shame. Flower vendors and restaurateurs discovered that celebrating a Western-style Valentine's Day increased their sales. Now the local florists promote one on the fourteenth of every month. One alley near our apartment is lined with shops offering turtles, fish, puppies, kittens, and birds as pets. On the next street over, most of the same creatures are offered as food. Whatever sells.

The Communist Party that sits atop this society has been both adaptable and rigid. In the nearly thirty years since

Deng Xiaoping introduced "Socialism with Chinese characteristics," aka capitalism under Communist political control, party leaders have adapted their way around one potentially ruinous difficulty after another. Even what the rest of the world sees as their most grievous mistake—the brutal crackdown at Tiananmen Square—was, from the regime's perspective, another success. Without it, they might well have been driven from power. And the international denunciation did not seriously slow the country's economic growth.

China's continued growth depends on businesses, both homegrown and foreign—but the conditions for the growth are still set by the commissars. Even in the relatively laissez-faire United States, the commissars of the Federal Reserve constantly try to find the interest-rate level that will let the economy grow without causing inflation. The equation the Chinese planners have to solve is much more complex, involving everything from pollution to currency controls to maintaining social order while exerting control.

As for pollution: How much can they allow without absolutely destroying the countryside? How much can they prohibit without hurting their big export businesses? Even if they want to clean up, can they enforce regulations that restrain polluting activities, when so many provincial authorities have so much graft to gain by approving the next freeway, toxic-waste dump, or coal-fired power plant?

As for trade frictions with the United States, the finance ministry has made a start toward wiggling its way out. By letting the yuan's value rise very slowly against the dollar, China has held down the price it pays for oil and other imported commodities that are priced in dollars—without overpricing its products in the U.S. markets. Senators Charles Schumer and Lindsey Graham frequently threaten to propose trade sanctions on China if it does not let the yuan's value rise much faster. Several economists I have interviewed here say that being forced to raise the yuan's value would actually be a huge victory for the Chinese economy. It would drive down import costs even further and would not do much to reduce exports to America, since many made-in-China goods are simply no longer manufactured in Europe or the United States. Can the Chinese officials work this negotiation to their benefit? My guess is yes.

A Western ambassador to China said that the thoroughgoing competence of the seemingly rigid central leadership is China's least appreciated strength. "They drive you crazy," he said, "but they get what they want done." The ambassador went down the list of fourteen countries bordering China and said, "In every case, they've built a reasonable relationship." A similar systematic effectiveness has characterized—so far—most of the country's economic and social policies.

Can the regime keep it up? Can China manage a giant-scale and much more repressive version of the social contract developed in Singapore? Lee Kuan Yew didn't call himself a benevolent despot in Singapore, but that's what he was. He offered prosperity and public order; he quashed dissent. That's the deal the Chinese leadership would offer the public—if it thought it had to offer explanations. Some people I've spoken with—mostly older people, and mostly ones who've lived in the West—say that of course the country will become more liberal as it becomes richer. Others—mainly younger ones, and those who've never left the country—say it's not necessarily so. "People get unhappy here when there are famines," a graduate student in Shanghai told me. "Otherwise we're not interested in politics."

Some philosophers, idealists, and ordinary citizens in China are taking risks to prove the student wrong. No one outside the country, and probably no one here, can tell how this process will come out. It turns on the leadership's skill, in the deepest sense: Can the leaders keep delivering what the country wants?

THE SECOND GREAT MYSTERY OF CHINA: WHAT IS THE CHINESE DREAM?

Holland has a culture, but it does not have a dream. There is no Canadian dream, or Finnish dream. If there is a Japanese dream, the women's version seems to be to escape their salaryman husbands, and the men's is to escape the offices where they toil for their salaries.

The two countries whose cultures can plausibly support the idea of a dream these days are the United States and China. The American dream covers something so elemental in human ambition that people from around the world think it applies to them. The Chinese dream reflects the unprecedented opportunities now open to at least some of this country's 1.3 billion people.

But what exactly will the Chinese dream mean? In three of

its aspects—for the individual, for the growing economy, and for Chinese culture and influence in the largest sense—the answer is not yet obvious, at least to me. How exactly the Chinese decide to define and pursue their dream will make a large difference to the rest of the world.

The question about individuals will be: Do they dream of anything more than making money? Americans I've met here tend to sound huffy about the total money-mindedness of today's rising urban Chinese. (Example of what they mean: A flashy Shanghainese woman in her twenties says, "I almost feel sorry for men these days. If they don't have an apartment, no chance of getting married. With no car—forget it!" Her bargaining position is strengthened by the ghoulish combination of China's one-child policy and its strong cultural preference that the lone child be a boy. Six boy babies are born and survive in China for every five girls. The imbalance is obvious among children on the street and noticeable even for young people now in their twenties, who were born after the one-child policy took hold.) Americans might seem the worst-positioned people on earth to complain about others' materialism. But I sense that beneath the tut-tutting is a question about what modern Chinese people are supposed to believe in at all. The years of the Cultural Revolution must have done something terrible to traditional family loyalties, and after the switch away from Maoist policies, there can't still be many true believers in a socialist ideal. In dramatic contrast to the United States, China has not been a deeply religious society. This leaves, for now, material improvement as a proxy for the meaning of life. Any generalization this broad obviously will be wrong about many individuals. But what, if anything, tomorrow's successful Chinese want beyond a bigger house and better car seems both important and impossible to know.

For the economy as a whole, the question is whether China dreams of matching the consumer-driven American model—or, like Japan before it, establishing a different model of long-term development. America's policy really boils down to the steady effort to give consumers more and more for less and less: deregulation, expanding free trade, embracing Wal-Mart and other chains. Japan's policy has boiled down to a steady effort to develop the country's manufacturing base, even if that leaves consumers paying higher prices and investors getting worse returns. Different systems, different goals—and Japan, despite its supposed "lost decade," has done a good job by its own lights. Its current account surplus, widely predicted to have evaporated by the mid-1990s, instead remains the largest in the world in absolute terms. Toyota, which during the "Japan as No. 1" years dreamed of being the world's leading automaker, will very soon be just that. American economists often scold Japan for its "foolish" emphasis on exports and surpluses at the cost of immediate consumer welfare. But no one who visits modern Japan will think its people look poor.

Based on the Maserati dealership around the corner and the amount of gold I see draped around rich women's necks, China is a good long-term candidate for the consumption-driven American model. But based on the steady flow of new regulatory orders from Beijing, the central authorities may have other ideas. For most of recorded history, China has been the strongest and richest country, not simply in Asia but in the world. Through sheer force of numbers, it seems likely someday to be the world's richest again. Another suspiciously common slogan is that all China really wants is to achieve a "Peaceful Rise in the World." We will see.

MR. ZHANG BUILDS HIS DREAM TOWN

MARCH 2007

The first time I met the Chinese tycoon Zhang Yue, he was showing guests the Versailles-style palace he had built on his estate. This was happening far from the coastal cities where so much of China's new wealth and glitter are on display. On a pleasant weekend last fall—"pleasant" with allowances for the opaque brown sky—Zhang (his family name) had invited three dozen fellow Chinese millionaires to join him at "Broad Town," the place where he lives and where Broad Air Conditioning, which he owns and runs, is based. Broad Town is on the outskirts of Changsha, a city known by few people outside China even though its population is roughly as large as New York's. In China, Changsha is famous as the capital of Hunan province and one of the places where the young Mao Zedong lived and worked. A twenty-three-foot-high statue of Mao, long a fixture in the city square, was recently re-covered in pure gold.

The event at Broad Town was a "luxury weekend" organized by Zhang and *Jet Asia-Pacific* magazine, a publication designed to introduce business jets and the associated lifestyle to "Asia-based High Net Worth Individuals" who are newly able to afford such products. Guests were flown in from across China, free, on private jets. On Saturday, foreign airplane manufacturers like Gulfstream, Bombardier, and Cessna displayed their latest products, and the French industrialist Serge Dassault, whose Falcon jets sell for tens of millions of dollars, described the joys of air travel without the airlines. This is largely a theoretical pleasure in China, where the People's Liberation Army still tightly controls airspace and discourages private flights. But a few private jets, among them one owned by Zhang, already crisscross the country, and China's current Five-Year Plan calls for airspace controls to be relaxed so a personal-airplane industry can arise. Niu Gensheng, the CEO of a group that controls one of China's largest dairy-products companies, was among the several guests from Inner Mongolia (charmingly, his family name means "cow"). He told *Jet Asia-Pacific* that the conference had helped him understand "the rationale behind the acquisition of such an essential business tool."

It was the aviation aspect of the event that got me there, by chance. I had agreed to help ferry a small Cirrus airplane that was part of the luxury weekend display from Changsha to its next destination, the Zhuhai Air Show in far southern China, near Macau. (The Cirrus was the same kind of plane I had owned and piloted in the United States.) But the weekend, I learned on arrival in Broad Town, was not just about airplanes. On Saturday evening, after the display, more than fifty guests and exhibitors dined at one long banquet table, in a marble-floored chamber that had been designed by Zhang's wife, Lai Yujing, and resembles a palazzo in Tuscany.

Then on Sunday morning, the guests took test drives in brand-new Porsche racing cars—bright yellow, red, lustrous black—along an improvised course made by closing off a public street adjoining Broad Town. A Hummer was also part of the fleet. As each car rolled in at the end of a circuit, a small clash of cultures could be observed. The Chinese millionaires, used to doing what they wanted the instant it occurred to them, would stride to the driver's side of the car, past anyone who happened to be waiting in line. Then a member of Porsche's professional-driver team would look for a tactful way to guide the guest to the passenger's side for a first, instructional run through the slalom cones and rapid-acceleration zones on the course.

After a few hours of driving, the guests went to Broad Town's Mediterranean Club, which had one wood-paneled room full of long, narrow felt-covered tables for snooker and a similar room with squarer, squatter felt-covered tables for playing pool. (Plus bowling alleys, a vast and modern indoor swimming pool, antique Chinese furniture and statues, and so forth; the facilities are open to all company employees.) A huge video screen at the back of the room ran footage about Sunseeker motor yachts, the maritime equivalent of private jets. On leather seats in the clubhouse's bar, the guests sat down to a tasting of $250-a-bottle French wine, poured by a young duo from Hong Kong. One of the wine merchants was British and looked like Prince William; as he described each wine in Chinese, his partner, a chic Chinese woman, went around the room pouring the wine. A few minutes into the tasting, the guests were summoned for lunch, and they carried along their glasses of 1994 Château Latour to enjoy with mouth-burning Hunan dishes.

After lunch, Zhang thanked the guests for coming and invited them to spend time seeing some of the other highlights of Broad Town: the 130-foot-high gold-colored replica of an Egyptian pyramid, for instance, or the life-size bronze statues of forty-three inspirational leaders from different eras and different cultures, from Confucius and Socrates to the Wright Brothers, Mahatma Gandhi, Rachel Carson, and Jack Welch. Later in the afternoon, one of the company helicopters came in for a landing not far from the Mediterranean Club. A group of guests ran toward the helipad to meet it—Zhang, in shirt and tie, running faster than anyone else, and grinning like a happy little boy.

The next time I met Zhang Yue was in Shanghai, at the China International Luxury Property Show, where resort properties from around the world—villas in France, ski lodges in Canada—were up for sale. His company was displaying its new line of home air conditioners in a small structure that got a large amount of attention because of two young female Broad employees who stood on its roof in skintight white bare-midriff outfits, playing electric violin and viola on numbers ranging from Bach to Grace Jones. (Or appearing to play: they were actually violin-synching—not that anyone cared.)

Zhang breezed smilingly past me and another foreigner who had come to see him. "Five minutes!" he said in Chinese, and spent the next half hour roaming through the display and pointing out to the dozen uniformed staff members every detail that could be improved. The Broad staffers stood at attention while listening, notebook in left hand and pen in right, as if trained in that pose—as I later learned they were.

A week later I saw Zhang Yue again, back at Broad Town. I had spent the previous night in the on-campus hotel, sans Internet or telephone, feeling remote from my known world. Then I ran into engineers from Trinidad, Russia, and Argentina who were in Broad Town for several weeks of lessons on maintaining Broad systems in their home countries. Like the 1,800 regular employees of the company, they were living next to the factory in Broad Town housing and eating three meals a day, free, in the company cafeteria, in a building with the English name Aspiration Theater. Unlike the 1,800, they were neither delighted by the prospect of Chinese food twenty-one times a week nor able to communicate easily in Chinese. "Remote!" a man from Trinidad scoffed when I told him the way I was feeling, and set off into an I'll-show-you-*remote* soliloquy.

The next morning, I toured the factory, where locomotive-sized institutional air conditioners were prepared for shipment to India, Germany, the United States, or one of forty other countries. I saw the company's "Aviation Division," where maintenance men kept Zhang's helicopter ready in case he wanted to make a trip. I saw the laboratory, and the warehouse, and the NORAD-style control room, where a team of technicians watched readouts from every large-scale Broad system installed in a hotel, office building, shopping mall, or airport anywhere in the world. While I watched, the display switched from a hotel in Manhattan to the international airport in Madrid to a new structure in Beijing.

Then it was time to interview the creator and owner of it all, whom I invariably heard referred to in Broad Town as "our chairman." Chairman Zhang strolled without formality or entourage into a tea-break room where I was sitting, slapped me on the back, and spent the next half hour grilling me, through an interpreter, about . . . airplanes. He loves flying, and he was the first person in China to buy a private jet. According to a Broad representative, he was also the first person in China to be certified as a private pilot, and while he rarely flies his airplanes himself anymore, he remains an aviation enthusiast. Now he wanted a new airplane. No—as an environmentalist, he *needed* a new airplane, one that was much more energy-efficient than the ones he now had. To be specific, he needed one that would go at least 300 miles an hour and get at least fifteen miles to a gallon of jet fuel. Zhang had lectured Dassault, the French aircraft baron, on the need to create such a plane. Zhang usually went by himself on business trips, so for efficiency he would be happy with a plane that had only two or three seats (plus one for a hired pilot). Since I had once written a book about airplanes, I should tell him which one to buy!

I delicately asked whether he needed such a plane now, or if he could wait two or three years for one of the many small jets currently being developed. Without waiting for translation he said, in Chinese, "Now! Now!" As I began to say (gulp) that no such plane existed at the moment, I saw his face cloud. So I backtracked and said I would call a friend at NASA who was the world's expert on exciting new aircraft, to see if he knew of one. "Fine!" said Zhang. "Let's call him now!" Well, it was 3:30 a.m. on the U.S. East Coast. Maybe we could wait an hour or two?

Airplanes deferred for the moment, Zhang spent half an hour talking about himself, his company, and his vision for China. Every second of that time, he was in motion around the room, talking as if dictating to scriveners. Zhang Yue is a short, very trim man, forty-six years old; his black hair appears undyed, and his face is youthful and smooth. "I have not taken a medicine in eighteen years!" he said at one point with pride. Nervous energy may be the key to his fitness. Like many Chinese nouveaux riches (I am told), he is impatient and indulged. Unlike many American plutocrats, he has no formality or stuffiness. I enjoyed being with him. Suddenly he decided that he'd had enough—and with a reminder that we'd meet that evening, after I called my NASA friend, he was gone.

China, like America, is too big, complicated, and contradictory to have any "typical" or representative character. Zhang Yue is no more representative of today's China than a fur merchant like John Jacob Astor or a press baron like William Randolph Hearst was representative of the America of his time. But certain prominent characters are interesting because they are so clearly *of* their culture's moment in history. Astor was of the era in which natural resources were being turned into fortunes, and those fortunes turned into social standing. Hearst built his fortune in the age of large urban markets and converted it, with mixed results, into political influence and the artistic legacy of his castle. Zhang is of the moment when China has opened the door to ambitious people with entrepreneurial plans. And to me he is more interesting than many others superficially like him, because he suggests an answer to one fundamental question about the China of the era to come. The question is what China will dream of as its dreams of money begin to be realized. Most people will be poor, far into the future. But tens of millions of Chinese are already able to think of more than just getting by. Zhang, it turns out, has more than making money and buying as-yet-undeveloped planes on his mind.

ZHANG OF THE BUSINESS WORLD

Depending on the rankings, Zhang Yue stands somewhere between twenty-fifth and fiftieth on the list of the richest people in China, with assets worth as much as $300 million; Broad Air Conditioning has no debt, and last year it had annual sales of about $300 million. His wealth does not appear to be based principally on political connections, which have obviously been crucial in the formation of other empires—in real estate, construction, and broadcasting, for example. Indeed, Broad has been discussed in Chinese business blogs, which I've seen in translation, as proof that a business can thrive while keeping government more or less at arm's length.

The company's English name is derived, perhaps too literally, from its Chinese name *Yuan Da*, which might also have been rendered as "expansive" or "spacious." The company's logo—the familiar @ sign, but with the *a* in the middle replaced by a lowercase *b*, for *Broad*—is elegant and eye-catching; Zhang designed it in 1990, before e-mail made the "at" symbol common. Among the six "Broad Values" that Zhang says must guide the company, one is "Don't pay bribes" and another is "Do pay taxes." (The others are environmental protection, respect for intellectual-property rights, no price gouging, and no predatory competition.)

Nor does Broad aim to beat its competitors with a lowball "China price" that manufacturers in developed countries cannot match. According to a quite respectful case study of Broad used at the Harvard Business School, the company's prospects have been closely tied to the technological niche that Zhang has insisted it occupy. Broad's specialty is a form of air-conditioning that uses less energy than conventional means. Broad did not invent the technology on which its business is based, but it did take the risk of investing heavily in an approach that companies in Japan, Korea, Europe, and North America had looked at and neglected.

The company and its CEO came to their current identities through an indirect route. Zhang grew up near Changsha, studied art in college, and began work as an interior decorator in southern China. His younger brother Jian trained as an engineer at Harbin Institute of Technology, in Manchuria. In the late 1980s, as Deng Xiaoping opened China seriously for business, Jian, in his mid-twenties, patented the invention that got the company started. This was a "pressure-free boiler" for factories, and its main selling point was that if anything went wrong, the boiler would collapse rather than explode. Such explosions were common in China; demand was brisk. Using the roughly $3,000 Zhang Yue had saved from his decorating company, the brothers went into business selling boilers and consulting on factory design.

By 1992, they had decided to concentrate on what is now Broad's entire business: "nonelectric refrigeration." The air conditioners most Americans are familiar with are compression coolers. They use electric power to compress a refrigerant such as Freon, and when the refrigerant expands, it cools the surrounding air. The nonelectric coolers instead use natural gas (or some other source of heat) to boil a lithium bromide solution, and when the vapors from that solution condense, they cool whatever is near them.

It sounds odd to use a flame to cool a building—and, indeed, when China's premier, Wen Jiabao, visited Broad Town in 2005, he asked several times to have the principle explained. A company pamphlet that lovingly commemorates this historic visit calls the premier's persistent curiosity a sure sign of his acumen. "If I spread a drop of alcohol on your hand, you will feel very cold," Zhang told Wen, describing part of the cooling process. The account continues: "The Premier nodded in understanding and said, 'Yes! Yes! For it evaporates and takes away the heat.' The Premier is a specialist indeed."

Zhang has never wavered from this technology, even when, in the early 2000s, market conditions temporarily turned against it and his sales force begged him to add normal, electric-powered air conditioners to Broad's offerings.

Its advantages all involve energy savings. Compared with typical compression systems, nonelectric air-conditioning as Broad makes it will always require less energy per unit of cooling, because when energy is converted from one form to another, some of it is lost. Electric-compression cooling requires more stages of conversion—fossil fuel to electricity at the power plant, electricity to mechanical power at the compressor, both stages very wasteful—than does using natural gas to boil liquid. Nonelectric cooling will also always be more adaptable to other sources of energy, since it is easier to apply a variety of heat sources, including solar power and biomass burning, to do the boiling than to use them to generate electricity in a remote plant and transmit it to the air-conditioning site. And this method of cooling helps reduce the costly peak loads imposed on the power grid, because natural gas is cheapest and most abundant in the summer, exactly when the demand for air-conditioning goes up. Indeed, since storing natural gas is expensive and difficult, in many countries the available gas is simply burned off—wasted—during the summer, when no one needs it for heating. In China, air-conditioning accounts for as much as 50 percent of the electric load during peak times in the summer. Zhang pointed out to me—as he has noted in countless speeches, and as is emphasized by the Harvard Business School case study—that with all of these advantages, his kind of air-conditioning can make both the electric and the natural-gas networks less wasteful while still keeping people cool in the summer. And while we're at it: the nonelectric systems use a relatively benign natural salt (lithium bromide) rather than using—and inevitably releasing—Freon and other chlorine-based products that erode the earth's ozone layer.

The company made its first big sale of air conditioners in China in 1992. As construction throughout China boomed, so did Broad's business—partly because installing the system required little paperwork or official approval compared with what was required for electric units, which would draw on the power grid. It succeeded overseas in India, Pakistan, and other countries with shaky electric systems, since the natural-gas-powered cooler would run during a brownout. "Japanese companies did poorly in markets like those, because their systems were designed for clean water and good management," Sean Wang, who handles Broad's international accounts, told me. "Ours were designed with the assumption of worse conditions and looser management."

Broad made its first American sale in 1999, a combined heating-cooling system at a medical center in downtown Boston. It pushed hard into the California market after the blackouts of 2000–2001, it equipped a community college in New Jersey, and it arrived in New York: Near Zhang's office is a large picture of a Broad cooler in a Con Edison plant in Manhattan. "Thomas Edison is our idol," Wang said. The company competed for, and won, Department of Energy contracts to demonstrate energy-saving techniques, notably a major project in Austin, Texas. It now has more than 200 installations in the United States, including at Fort Bragg and other military bases, and many hundreds more around the world, including in the new airport facilities in Madrid, Athens, and Bangkok.

In 2001, '02, '04, and '05, Broad was named one of the "20 Most Admired Companies in China" by China's *Economic Observer* weekly. I thought of asking Zhang, "What happened in 2003?" But I only thought it.

ZHANG: UTOPIAN OR TYRANT?

The first time I was in an office building at Broad Town, a European friend who has lived in China for years nudged me and asked, "What don't you see?" I looked around and realized: I didn't see piles of junk. There were no scrap papers, cigarette butts, half-empty teacups, or other debris on the Broad Town desks, which made it different from other places I had seen in China. What was true in the office was true of the factory as well: no heaps of spare parts or scrap metal, no workers holding welding guns while standing barefoot, no oily rags looking as if they were about to burst into flame. What I had seen in many other Chinese work sites fit the motto, "If it's worth doing, it's worth doing sloppily." But when I saw a gardener kneeling on one of Broad Town's sweeping lawns and resodding a small plot of grass practically blade by blade, I realized: This is like Japan!

Those would be fighting words in much of China, so let me be precise: The people working at Broad Town seemed not just to be holding jobs but to have been made into a culture and team. Japan's thoroughgoing organization of people into large teams—the Mitsubishi team, the Toyota team—often seems like a peacetime military. At Broad Town the connection is more explicit. New recruits go through a ten-day session of literal boot camp, wearing military-style outfits and living in barracks on the grounds. They run in platoons through Broad Town's streets in fatigues, behind an instructor carrying a unit flag. Many of the blog-world concerns about Broad involve recruits who drop out during the training—or are summarily dismissed for versions of "bad attitude."

After demobilization into the regular workforce, employees are like an army in mufti. They eat, work, and sleep on the base—I mean, the factory grounds. They are roused each morning at 6:00 for physical training before the workday begins. Zhang and his wife and son live at Broad Town, too, as do his parents, in houses tucked behind the fishpond that helps supply the company cafeteria. White-collar workers, male and female, wear a blue-blazer uniform every day, as does Zhang. Factory workers wear royal blue uniforms with their employee number stenciled in large digits down one leg. Every Monday morning the workforce musters for the raising of the national and company flags. When I asked Sean Wang about the clean factories and overall air of control, he said, "We want to solve problems at their root." He was talking about how a little bit of dirt in the factory could lead to big, expensive problems later on, but the point seemed to apply more generally. It was a one-company illustration of what former Singaporean Prime Minister Lee Kuan Yew and others have called the Asian social bargain: less individual latitude, more collective success.

I heard from a former factory worker that pay for blue-collar workers, nearly all of them male, starts at 1,200 yuan per month, or about $150* [about $175 in late 2008]. That's not bad by Chinese factory standards—especially considering that Changsha is a low-cost area, and Broad workers get their food and housing free. I've visited factories near Shanghai and Guangzhou where monthly wages started at 900 yuan. Zhou Wei, of Broad, declined to comment on pay levels in the company, but I heard that white-collar workers started at around 2,000 yuan per month. In theory, Chinese law requires companies to pay overtime to anyone working more than forty hours in a week. Some managers of North American–, Japanese-, or European-owned companies with Chinese plants have mentioned to me that they obey this rule. It hardly ever comes up in discussions with companies from mainland China, Taiwan, or Singapore. At Broad the rule seems to be "Work till the job is done." I met some former employees who said that they typically had two days off per month; often worked till midnight; and survived by shoveling down food as quickly as they could and then using the rest of their lunch and dinner breaks, two hours apiece, for sleep. They weren't complaining: this is modern China.

As will be obvious by now, there are things both admirable and creepy about this utopia. In every way possible, Zhang has isolated the culture of Broad Town from influences other than his own. He has no public shareholders to second-guess his choices—whether to stick to environmentally friendly

---

* Dollar equivalents throughout are current as of original publication time, with $1 worth 7.5 to 8 RMB. Values as of late 2008, with $1 equals 6.8 RMB, are shown in brackets.

products or to build a pyramid—nor even bankers holding debt. He has distanced the company from governmental control as much as any Chinese company owner can. His workers are physically distant from the distractions of Changsha—and that city itself is distant from the thriving metropolises of the coast. The same blogs that complain about imposed cultlike behavior at Broad acknowledge that the jobs pay well enough that plenty of new applicants are always willing to put on military uniforms and live their lives at Broad Town.

The positive aspect of this invented world is its ambition for something more than sheer efficiency and success. The entire workforce also musters for musical events. Many employees play musical instruments, and apparently all can, or do, sing. On December 31, 1999, Zhang had all of his workers stand in front of the then half-finished Versailles to be photographed singing in the new millennium. (The palace now serves as a "management training center" for meetings and seminars; the pyramid's interior is being fitted out as an environmental museum.) The inspirational sayings carved on nearly every wall could sound like corporate boilerplate. From the founder of Toyota: "There is no boat that cannot be sunk." (Moral: Don't let up.) But the walls also bear sayings from Abraham Lincoln and other noncorporate figures. Among those honored with statues are Winston Churchill, the Chinese poet Li Bai, and Martin Luther King, Jr. Zhang has not forgotten his background as an artist, and he is renowned for fussing over every design detail of every feature of Broad Town.

When I asked him a more polite version of what any visitor would wonder—What is the deal with the pyramid?—Zhang said, "Our products are to make people comfortable and happy. If our employees are comfortable and happy, that will affect their work ethic and their professionalism." He said that good food matters—and the food at Broad Town is good. So does a visually pleasant environment—and most vistas in this controlled landscape are pleasant. "Many companies in China are looking only for the short-term profit," he said in conclusion. "Some of our expenditures are not directly for manufacture and sales, but our vision is long-term, and we believe that indirectly they will increase manufacture and sales." And even if the steps don't pay off, in the end it's his company, and like utopians before him, he seems to consider it another work of art.

ZHANG AND INCONVENIENT TRUTHS

If I had asked my European friend what he was seeing but not noticing at Broad Town, the answer should have been: wood. Polished, attractive wood shows up in every structure. Clean, gleaming wood floors and beams in a lovely Japanese house, built (for no apparent reason) as part of a "Global Village" of housing styles from around the world. Wooden parquet floors and walls in a gymnasium for badminton and Ping-Pong. Wooden furniture in many of the offices. Dark wood paneling in the Mediterranean Club. Wood-block flooring throughout. If China was ever rich in timber resources, it certainly is not now. Why should a heavy-industry facility use so much expensive wood? Because it was free. All of the wood was recycled from shipping pallets and packing crates coming into the factory. Where it came from before that is another matter, but once it got to Broad Town, it was carefully reprocessed and reused—all at the insistence of Zhang Yue.

There is a showboat aspect to Broad Town's recycling effort—every person I met there told me the story of the packing crates. And the Porsches roaring through town over the luxury weekend did not quite fit Zhang's message that people should be conscious of their environmental impact at all times. But in fairness, when the United Nations Environment Program held a forum at Broad Town in 2003, Zhang argued that worldwide, systematic changes—in energy, packaging, and transportation—were essential so consumers could "enjoy a comfortable yet moderate life." And when we finally reached my friend from NASA, around 6:30 a.m. EST, Zhang grilled him (through an interpreter) about the most efficient engines on the market—and lit up when he heard about a radically more efficient airplane being made in Austria. His company got its start partly because China was growing too fast for its own electric grid. Over the last decade he has read constantly about environmental problems and has come up with serious-sounding proposals for what his company, his country, and the world can do.

Solar-energy collectors are everywhere in Broad Town. Part of boot-camp indoctrination is training employees about environmental issues. When the company sells a cooling unit, it also offers guidance on reducing demand for air-conditioning. "For years the Chinese government focused only on economic development, but now they say that the environment and the economy should both be stressed,"

Zhang told me. "But really the environment needs to be in first place, and economic growth in fourth." Not seeing the trap, I asked what should come second and third. "The environment, and the environment!" he said. "The real measure of our economic progress is the life people can live, and the [gross domestic product] does not measure that." He observed that a ton of dirty coal might bring 120 yuan in profit—but recent studies have shown that a ton of coal costs at least 200 yuan in medical care for inhabitants of the bleak, cancer-ridden mining towns. "Any primary-school child can see what's wrong with that," Zhang said, "but our economists can't."

For another international conference on the environment, Zhang prepared a captivating and unintentionally revealing document called "The World in 2015." Part of it is quiet Chinese triumphalism: the world's largest trading zone will be in Asia; the international currency will be not the U.S. dollar but the Asian dollar; the world's most popular movie will be a drama set in ancient China. The world's most profitable and admired company will not be one that sells computers or airplanes or oil but one that quietly economizes on energy use around the world, starting with new air-conditioning systems. "This company still has little reputation, for they have done those things others don't care about. . . . It doesn't matter that people may not know the name of this company, but they should know it is a Chinese company."

The conclusion of the imagined history involves a historic UN speech by another of Zhang's idols: "Albert Gore, sixty-seven years old, walked slowly to the platform. This old man, who became secretary-general of the UN one year ago, has a dull look in his eyes." Why had no one heeded his warnings when there had been time? Why did the world keep building more coal and nuclear plants, instead of noticing what was happening to its climate and learning to conserve? "Choked with sobs, Secretary [Gore] cannot speak." At last he finds his voice and challenges mankind, in the final words of Zhang's essay, "to choose the establishment of the new moral ideal with higher standards."

Subtle? No. Consistent with every detail of Zhang's daily life? Probably not. But as an indication that more than pure moneymaking is under way, it is worth noticing. China will bring more than mere commerce to the world.

WIN IN CHINA!

APRIL 2007

You think TV is bad in America, and then you watch it someplace else. For all of its defects, American TV generally has high production values—attractive people to look at, sets and staging that don't seem homemade—and it is often the place where new ideas get their start, just before they become worldwide clichés.

Right now the curse of Chinese TV, apart from its being state-controlled and de facto censored, is the proliferation of stupid, low-budget reality shows. The oddest reality show I've come across while channel surfing was a World's Strongest Man–type contest between teams of midgets. The cruelest, put on by the state-owned China Central Television (CCTV), pitted young families against one another in elimination events. Each family team had three members—father, mother, elementary-school-aged child—and did coordinated stunts. Three families survived each show to appear in future rounds, and three were sent home, the children inconsolable and the husbands and wives looking daggers at each other.

Fortunately there is also a best Chinese reality show, or at least one that my wife and I followed avidly through its increasingly suspenseful Tuesday night episodes last year. We first heard of *Ying Zai Zhongguo*, or *Win in China*, from a Chinese American friend, Baifang Schell, who was involved in the production. We became so interested that in December we traveled to Beijing to be in the audience at CCTV's cavernous main studio for the live final episode, in which one grand champion was chosen from five remaining contestants. Like many other Chinese reality shows, this one featured a segment known by the English letters "PK." This means nothing to most English speakers (penalty kick?), but it is widely recognized in China as meaning "Player Kill" in online games.

The PK stage of *Win* served the function of the tribal council in *Survivor* or the boardroom in *The Apprentice*: After a contest or judges' assessment each week, two of that episode's competitors ended up pitted against each other in a three-minute lightning elimination. This is PK, in which one opponent issues a question, challenge, or taunt, and the other tries to answer, outwit, and provoke the first. Once done speaking, a competitor slams a hand down on a big button, stopping his or her own clock (as with a chess-match timer) and starting the opponent's. Faster and faster, each contestant tries to manage the time so as to get the very last word. The audience gasps, cheers, and roars with laughter at the gibes— and at the end, one contestant is "killed," as determined by audience vote or a panel of judges. Even if you can barely follow the language, it's exciting.

But something else distinguishes *Win in China*—not just from the slew of other reality shows but also from its American model, *The Apprentice*, with Donald Trump. "The purpose of

The Apprentice was very functional," Wang Lifen, the producer and on-camera host of the show, told me (in English) shortly after the final episode. "There's some job that already exists, and Donald Trump is just looking for somebody to fill it, while providing entertainment." Wang said that she had higher ambitions for her show: "We want to teach values. Our dream for the show is to enlighten Chinese people and help them realize their own dreams." Having seen the program and talked with contestants and compared it with some superficially similar Chinese reality shows, I don't scoff at what she said.

The didactic and uplifting ambitions of the show could be considered classically Chinese, the latest expression of a value-imprinting impulse that stretches from the Analects of Confucius to the sayings of Chairman Mao. Or they could be considered, like the Horatio Alger novels of young, muscular America, signs of an economy at an expansive moment when many people want to understand how to seize new opportunities. Either way, the particular message delivered by the show seems appropriate to China at this stage of its growth. Reduced to a moral, *Win in China* instructs Chinese people that they have chances never open to their compatriots before—but also that, as one contestant told me at the end of the show, "The only one I can rely on is myself."

Wang Lifen moved from Beijing to Washington, D.C., in the fall of 2004, for a one-year fellowship at the Brookings Institution. She was then in her late thirties and was an influential figure in CCTV's news division, where she had created and produced documentaries and talk shows. By the time she returned to CCTV a year later, she was ready to act on a question she'd asked while watching American TV: What would an improved, Sinified version of *The Apprentice* look like?

It would be Chinese in being huge. There would be thousands of initial candidates, with entry open to any adult "of Chinese origin" anywhere in the world. More than 100 (versus *The Apprentice*'s 18) would have a serious chance to compete on camera for the prize. The nature of that prize indicated why *Win in China* could seem more American than its American model. Instead of a job and a paycheck within a Trump-style empire, Wang offered seed money for new entrepreneurial ventures—and for more than just one contestant. By Chinese standards, the sums were enormous. The ultimate victor would receive 10 million yuan, or nearly $1.3 million. The runner-up would get 7 million yuan, and the three other finalists would get 5 million yuan apiece. With other prizes and incentives, the money the show was offering came to nearly $4 million.

This would be large even for a U.S. show, but the source of the prizes was even more unusual. Wang raised the money not from sponsors or the network but from individual investors in China—for instance, Andrew Yan, of Softbank Asia Infrastructure Fund, who had recently been named "Venture Capitalist of the Year" by the China Venture Capital Association. Yan and a few other investors, including Kathy Xu, of Capital Today, and Hugo Shong, of the U.S.-based company IDG, put up the pool of prize money—in return for a 50 percent share in the real-world businesses the winning contestants would use it to create or expand. Twenty percent would belong to the contestants, and 15 percent to the show's production company. The remaining 15 percent would go by "lucky draw" to viewers who had voted for candidates, via mobile-phone text messages, during the show's run. In effect, the many weeks of the program (33 episodes were shown in all, some live) amounted to a drawn-out, public version of a pitch to venture capitalists (the investors) from entrepreneurs seeking their backing (the contestants). Every week, contestants would be put through some kind of quiz or business-oriented team challenge that would whittle their numbers down. Wang had an additional hope for this process: that it would give viewers practical tips on starting businesses of their own.

Within a few months of her return, Wang had rounded up the financial backing, gotten the show on CCTV's schedule, and begun the hunt for candidates. (China is a timeless civilization and so on, but today's business deals can happen very fast.) Her team posted Web notices and placed ads in 20 newspapers around the country, asking potential entrepreneurs to send in résumés and business plans. In March 2006, the top 3,000 (!) files were sent to screening teams, which reduced the pool to about 500. Interviews of at least 15 minutes apiece then produced 108 semifinalists—an auspicious number, because of the "108 heroes" (also known variously as the "108 bandits" and "108 generals") of a famed uprising in the Shandong mountains a thousand years ago.

All of the 108 came to Beijing at their own expense and made a mass climb of the Great Wall, along with the investors, producers, and judges, to build team spirit for the challenges ahead. Then, in one televised debut episode, the 108 were divided into two big teams and winnowed down to a field of 36, based on their performance in a computerized simulation of business decisions. Meanwhile, all 108 were given off-camera seminars on finance, personnel management, and other skills each would need as an entrepreneur.

Through the next stage, the 36 survivors appeared in groups of four before panels of judges that included prominent Chinese business and academic figures. The best-known was Jack Ma, cofounder and CEO of China's dominant e-commerce site, Alibaba. Each contestant had two minutes to present his or her business plan (three women were among the 36), after which the judges would begin the interrogation. What about holes in the plan? What was Plan B, if the sales projections didn't pan out? Why was this plan better than other candidates'? Often the questions came from investors whose own money was at stake.

On September 5, the producers held a reception at CCTV's Beijing headquarters for 6,000 guests: contestants, friends and family, press, and business dignitaries. The 12 finalists were announced—and then taken away to the Huang Yuan hotel in Beijing, where they would spend the next four weeks being filmed competing.

The seven further weeks of the show, which took the 12 contestants down to the five who would compete in the finale we went to, drew an audience that grew to 5 million (considered large for this "serious" a show), were discussed avidly in numerous blogs, and had a structure more or less familiar from American reality shows. The competitive pattern was essentially like that of *The Apprentice*: The 12 contestants were divided into two teams, which then competed against each other in some real-world business task—selling life insurance, raising money for charity, improvising a solution to some other business problem. Members of the winning team got to come back for the next episode. Members of the losing team went through various other assessments that included a final PK. Based on how the pair sounded when debating, a panel of judges would send one or the other home.

All the contestants were interesting, but we found ourselves rooting for four. Zhou Jin, one of two women among the final 12, was general manager of an advertising agency, and her project was to develop new labor-training services. She was seven months pregnant when the competition began and was granted permission for a brief absence from on-camera segments, but then fought her way back into consideration with strong performances. Ms. Zhou had a sassy air and, as best I could judge from others' reactions, a sharp tongue. She had a lot of backing in blogs because of the way she handled her pregnancy.

We came to think of Song Wenming as the social-conscience candidate. He was a mild-looking, baby-faced man in his early thirties from Anhui province, an impoverished area, many of whose people end up as illegal migrant workers in the big coastal cities. Song himself had earned an M.B.A. and held a job with a big international accounting firm. He resigned and, with two friends, started an employment firm to match Anhui people with jobs. His business plan was to expand these operations with new capital.

Zhou Yu was jokingly called "Wolf" or "Wild Wolf" by his competitors, but we thought of him as "Country Boy." He was a tall, rangy 35-year-old with a buzz cut who had worked for years in the clothing business, and his business plan was to expand factories for lingerie and other ladies' apparel. In manner, he was much earthier than most of the other contestants—barking out remarks, grimacing, predictably losing his temper at some point in each show. Among the final 12, he was the only one not to have gone past high school, and during PKs he talked about the limits of book learning and the value of the school of hard knocks. He was a favorite in mobile-phone voting.

Then there was Zhao Yao, who struck us as the smoothest of the candidates. He grew up in Beijing but now lives in Los Angeles, having been based in America since 1995. He'd left China to get an M.B.A. at the University of Wyoming, and then tried to set up what he later described to me as his "Wyoming-based self-service tour-planning company." After work-permit problems, he'd moved to California, where he was a computer programmer, an accountant, and a business consultant. He dreamed of bringing the "direct-response marketing" business to China. Direct-response marketing is the polite name for the infomercial business, and Zhao planned to set up the infrastructure—call centers, payment systems, customer service—that would allow the George Foreman Grill, for example, to be sold on TV in China (except here it would be the Jackie Chan Grill).

Week by week, our candidates survived, until the last episode before the live finale. Zhou Jin, the woman, and Zhao Yao, the Californian, were both on the team that lost that week's competition, and they were pitted against each other in the final PK. One or the other would go down! Their debate was relatively high-road, each pointing out his or her own strengths rather than the other's weaknesses. Ms. Zhou looked shocked when the judges' result was announced: She would go on to the finals, and Zhao was out. This seemed shocking because Zhao had seemed, probably even to her, such a golden-boy candidate. When the series was over, I asked him, in English, how he interpreted his elimination. "If I had just spoken my mind, here is what I would have said before the verdict," he told me. "I would have told the judges, 'I don't think I've given you any reason to eliminate me. But the lady hasn't given you any reason to eliminate her.' Under the circumstances—her being pregnant, the struggles of a young mom, the public support—you should just take me out.'" As they did.

Everything about the live final show was meant to be spectacular. Most episodes had three judges; this time there were 11. In addition to famous investors like Jack Ma and Hugo Shong, there were other prominent business figures, like Niu Gensheng, head of one of China's leading dairy companies. Introduced separately, and given the right to make the final selection, were the heads of the two most respected firms in all of China: Lenovo, the leading computer company, and Haier, which has a high reputation for quality and which absolutely dominates the domestic "white goods" market for refrigerators, washing machines, and so on. *Win* publicists said this was the first time the two CEOs, Yang Yuanqing of Lenovo and Zhang Ruimin of Haier, had made a joint appearance.

The two finalists who were not among our candidates were the first two eliminated in PKs. Then things got serious. Ms. Zhou, Song "Social Conscience" Wenming, and Zhou "Wild Wolf" Yu answered questions from the judges—and mobile-phone votes showed that Song had done best of the three. Thus the two Zhous had to face off in a PK, whose drama was apparent even if you didn't understand what they were saying. In an earlier round of questions, all five candidates had had to explain their greatest weakness. Mr. Zhou said that he had a bad temper—but that passion was a good thing in a leader! And so, he helpfully pointed out, was the kind of education you couldn't get from books. For her part, Ms. Zhou said that her attention was always flitting from subject to subject; on the other hand, that kind of alert eye could help in running a business.

During the PK, it was as if Ms. Zhou was trying to make Mr. Zhou explode. "You are avoiding my questions; maybe you don't have enough learning to answer." "They call you the 'Wolf,' it would be better for the Wolf to stay in the wilderness." After Mr. Zhou (unwisely) mentioned that he was thinking of going back to school, she dug in: "Even if you get the diploma, it won't mean real skills." After inserting each of her barbs, Ms. Zhou would slap her PK button with a smile at the audience and a little rise of her eyebrows. Wild Wolf would splutter and yell, slamming his fist onto his button, and finally getting a near-ovation from the crowd when he said, "You question my skills, but I am standing here tonight! That should be proof enough for anyone!" He also had the last words, which were: "I'll talk to you later!"

As it turned out, in trying to provoke the Wolf, Ms. Zhou ended up mortally wounding them both. The judges declared him the victor over her in this PK—one said later that he was "like China itself, from a poor background, still crude, but proud of its rise"—and so she had to sit down. But in the anti-climactic final choice between Mr. Zhou and Song Wenming, the M.B.A., Zhou's fiery and uncontrolled outbursts during his PK with Ms. Zhou proved his undoing. All 11 judges spoke, many saying that passion was great, but you needed a steady hand to build an enterprise. Song Wenming was nothing if not steady. The Haier and Lenovo CEOs glanced at each other and gave the winner's name: Song Wenming.

What had it all meant? I got in touch with our four contestants later on, Zhao Yao in person when he visited Shanghai and the others by e-mail through a translator. Each made veiled and provocative comments about the contest itself. When I asked Ms. Zhou about differences between the contest as she experienced it and what viewers saw on TV, she said she could not give any details, "because of traditional Chinese values" of discretion. "All I can say is that the exposure of the most repulsive side of human nature by us—if there was any, because of the award—did not, fortunately, appear in front of the audience." (She added that some altruistic moments had also escaped capture.) She said that she had often felt "condescension and suspicion" toward her talents from others on the show because of her gender, but hoped that her success would be encouraging for Chinese women in general. ("And after all, the United States only now has its first woman speaker of the House.")

When I asked Zhao Yao whether his life was different now, he began in stentorian tones—"The impact of my involvement in the show has been profound"—and then started laughing and said, "I am taking the tone promoted by the show, enthusiastic and assertive!" He said that becoming famous enough to be recognized on the street had been of great practical benefit, since a real venture capitalist had now offered him funding. "I do wonder if the actors in U.S. reality shows would be expected to iron our own shirts and wash our own socks while encamped in a hotel room for a month," he added. "Maybe they do—I only know that's what we did."

Zhou Yu, the Wolf, said he was glad to have been the people's champion. He had also learned that his wife was now referred to as "Wolf's Wife." Song Wenming, the winner, said that he had grown exasperated at times but had been confident he'd do well as long as he could just be himself before the judges. In indirect or open ways, all of them made clear that what was shown on-screen had been trimmed, rearranged, and highlighted to seem more dramatic. "Maybe this is the 'reality' that reality TV is introducing us to!" Zhao Yao said.

About one point all of them sounded utterly sincere: their hope that the program would encourage more people in China to start their own businesses. Song Wenming put it in historic terms: Its age-old ethic of stability was part of the reason China had fallen so far behind Western countries, and even now, "Chinese culture does not facilitate creativity very much." He hoped the show would introduce the "positive power" of entrepreneurship. Ms. Zhou said she hoped potential entrepreneurs would learn the importance of both perseverance and passion. There was much more in the same vein.

"I have a close friend on the staff of a state-owned company," Wang Lifen, the show's producer, told me. "After the final episode, she called and said, 'I have to quit my work unit and my company! I have to be an entrepreneur, because I want a new life.'" Women must retire from state-owned companies in China by 55; men by 60. "No one can provide for the next stage of life but me," Wang's friend told her.

According to Wang, a "minister-level" official in the Chinese government called the head of CCTV when the series was over and asked, "How can we make everyone watch this show?" (In China, this might not be a purely rhetorical question.) As a start, CCTV has renewed the show for two more seasons. "There is no religion in China, so it is very important to promote the right kind of values," Wang said. "Today for our society, the entrepreneur can be our hero."

"Hero" might be going too far, but the participants on *Win* seem to have been received in the press and blogs as modern Chinese role models. Having listened to their dreams and followed their on-screen contests, I cannot help wishing all of them well. Even more, I hope China's development is such that their show is eventually looked back on the way Horatio Alger's *Luck and Pluck* is: as an unsubtle and perhaps oversincere effort to teach people the rules of peaceful prosperity. I hope it doesn't eventually become another bit of evidence about the Chinese bubble: the way people behaved when they thought the good times would always go on.

CHINA MAKES,
THE WORLD TAKES

JULY 2007

Half the time I have spent in China I have spent in factories. At least that's how it feels—and it's a feeling I sought. The factories where more than 100 million Chinese men and women toil, and from which cameras, clothes, and every other sort of ware flow out to the world, are to me the most startling and intense aspect of today's China. For now, they are also the most important. They are startling above all in their scale. I was prepared for the skyline of Shanghai and its 240-mph Maglev train to the airport, and for the nonstop construction, dust, and bustle of Beijing. Every account of modern China mentions them. But I had no concept of the sweep of what has become the world's manufacturing center: the Pearl River Delta of Guangdong province (the old Canton region), just north of Hong Kong. That one province might have a manufacturing workforce larger than America's. Statistics from China are largely guesses, but Guangdong's population is around 90 million. If even one-fifth of its people hold manufacturing jobs, as seems likely in big cities, that would be 18 million—versus 14 million in the entire United States.

One facility in Guangdong province, the famous Foxconn works, sits in the middle of a conurbation just outside Shenzhen, where it occupies roughly as much space as a major airport. Some 240,000 people (the number I heard most often; estimates range between 200,000 and 300,000) work on its assembly lines, sleep in its dormitories, and eat in its company cafeterias. I was told that Foxconn's caterers kill 3,000 pigs each day to feed its employees. The number would make sense—it's one pig per 80 people, in a country where pigs are relatively small and pork is a staple meat (I heard no estimate for chickens). From the major ports serving the area, Hong Kong and Shenzhen harbors, cargo ships left last year carrying the equivalent of more than 40 million of the standard 20-foot-long metal containers that end up on trucks or railroad cars. That's one per second, round the clock and year-round—and it's less than half of China's export total. What's in the containers that come back from America? My guess was, dollars; in fact, the two leading shipborne exports from the United States to China, by volume, are scrap paper and scrap metal, for recycling.

And the factories are important, for China and everyone else. Someday China may matter internationally mainly for the nature of its political system or for its strategic ambitions. Those are significant even now, of course, but China's success in manufacturing is what has determined its place in the world. Most of what has been good about China over the past generation has come directly or indirectly from its factories. The country has public money with which to build roads, houses, and schools—especially roads. The vast population in the countryside has what their forebears acutely lacked, and peasants elsewhere today still do: a chance at paying jobs, which means a chance to escape rural poverty. Americans complain about cheap junk pouring out of Chinese mills, but they rely on China for a lot that is not junk, and whose cheap price is important to American industrial and domestic life. Modern consumer culture rests on the assumption that the nicest, most advanced goods—computers, audio systems, wall-sized TVs—will get cheaper year by year. Moore's law, which in one version says that the price of computing power will be cut in half every 18 months or so, is part of the reason, but China's factories are a big part, too.

Much of what is threatening about today's China also comes from its factories. Many people inside China, and nearly everyone outside, can avoid the direct effects of the country's political controls. It is much harder to avoid its pollution. The air in Chinese cities is worse than I expected, and because the pollution affects so many people in such a wide range of places, it is more damaging than London's, Manchester's, or Pittsburgh's in their worst, rapidly industrializing days. The air pollution comes directly from the steelworks, cement plants, and other heavy-industry facilities that are helping the country prosper, and indirectly from the electric power plants that keep everything running. (Plus more and more cars, though China still has barely one-thirtieth as many per capita as the United States.) The sheer speed and volume with which factories and power plants across China increase their output of soot and gases make the country's air-pollution problems the world's. The heightened competition for oil, ore, and other commodities to feed the factories affects other nations, as do slapdash standards of food purity and safety, which may have led to tainted worldwide supplies of animal food. The ultimate fear in the developed world, of course, is that as China creates millions of new factory jobs, unknown millions will lose such jobs in America, Canada, Germany, and even Japan.

But these factories are both surprising and important in a less obvious, though also fundamental, sense. Almost nothing about the way they work corresponds to the way they are discussed in the United States. America's political debates about the "China opportunity" and, even more, the "China threat" seem distant, theoretical, and imprecise from the perspective of the factories where the outsourcing and exporting occur. The industrialists from the United States, Europe, or Japan who are deciding how much of their production to move to China talk about the process in very different terms from those used in American political discussion. One illustration: The artificially low value of China's currency, relative to the dollar, comes near the top of American complaints about Chinese trade policy. (The currency is the yuan renminbi—literally, "people's money"—or RMB.) This is more like the eighth or tenth issue that comes up when business officials discuss the factories they are opening in one country and closing in another. And when it does come up, the context is usually whether the RMB's rise will force a company to put its next factory not in China's crowded coastal region but someplace with even lower costs, like the remote interior provinces, where salaries are lower and commercial space is cheaper—or perhaps Vietnam or Cambodia.

So too with complaints about Chinese government subsidies for exporting industries, widespread abuse of intellectual property, and even "slave labor" inside the vast factories. Some of these complaints are well-founded, others are not; but even if all were true, they would misdescribe and undervalue what is going on here. Talking about Chinese industrial growth, Americans are in the position of nineteenth-century Europeans who acted as if America's industrial rise could be explained simply by its vast natural resources and its exploitation of immigrant and slave labor, plus its very casual attitude toward copyright and patent laws protecting foreign, mainly British, books and inventions. (Today, Americans walk the streets of China and see their movies, music, software, and books sold everywhere in cheap pirate versions. A century and a half ago, Charles Dickens walked the streets of young America and fumed to see his novels in cheap pirate versions.) All those factors played their part, but they were not the full story of America's rise—nor do the corresponding aspects of modern China's behavior fully explain what China has achieved.

I can't pretend to know the complete story of China's industrial rise. But I can describe what I have seen, and the main way it has changed my mind.

Large-scale shifts in economic power have effects beyond the purely economic. Americans need not be hostile toward China's rise, but they should be wary about its eventual effects. The United States is the only nation with the scale and power to try to set the terms of its interaction with China rather than just succumb. So starting now, Americans need to consider the economic, environmental, political, and social goals they care about defending as Chinese influence grows.

The consideration might best start from the point about which I've changed my mind: So far, America's economic relationship with China has been successful and beneficial—and beneficial for both sides. Free trade may not always be good for all participants, and in the long run, trade with China may hold perils for the United States. But based on what I have seen in China, and contrary to what I expected before I came, so far it is working as advertised. Before thinking about what should be changed, Americans should appreciate what has gone right. A good place to begin that story is Shenzhen.

HOW IT WORKS: THE VIEW FROM THE FOUR POINTS

Each time I went to breakfast at the Sheraton Four Points in Shenzhen, I felt as if I were in a movie. I had a specific scene in mind: the moments aboard a U.S. aircraft carrier in a typical World War II movie when the flight crews gather in the wardroom to discuss the mission on which they're about to embark.

The morning crowd at the Four Points has that same sort of anticipatory buzz. Shenzhen, which is the part of China immediately north of Hong Kong and its "New Territories," did not exist as a city as recently as Ronald Reagan's time in the White House. It was a fishing town of 70,000 to 80,000 people, practically unnoticeable by Chinese standards. Today's other big coastal manufacturing centers, such as Xiamen, Guangzhou, Hangzhou, and Shanghai, have been consequential Chinese cities for centuries. Not Shenzhen. Its population has grown at least a hundredfold in the past 25 years—rather than merely tripled or quadrupled, as in other cities. It is roughly as populous as New York, like many Chinese cities I keep coming across. Shenzhen has scores of skyscrapers and many, many hundreds of factories.

The story of Shenzhen's boom is in a sense the first chapter in modern China's industrialization. "During the founding period, Shenzhen people were bold and resolute in smashing the trammels of the old ideas," reads the English version of the city's history, as recounted in Shenzhen's municipal museum in an odd, modern-Chinese combination of Maoist bombast and supercapitalist perspective. "With the market-oriented reforms as the breakthrough point, they shook off the yoke of the planned economy, and gradually built up new management systems."

What all this refers to is the establishment, in the late summer of 1980, of Shenzhen as a "special economic zone," where few limits or controls would apply and businesses from around the world would be invited to set up shop. Shenzhen was attractive as an experimental locale, not just because it was so close to Hong Kong, with its efficient harbor and airport, but also because it was so far from Beijing. If the experiment went wrong, the consequences could be more easily contained in this southern extremity of the country. Nearly every rule that might restrict business development was changed or removed in Shenzhen. Several free-trade processing zones were established, in which materials and machinery coming in and exports going out would be exempt from the usual duties or taxes.

Modern Shenzhen has traits that Americans would associate with a booming Sunbelt city—transient, rough, unmannered, full of opportunity—and that characterized Manchester, Detroit, Chicago, Los Angeles at their times of fastest growth. Newspapers that cover Shenzhen are full of stories of drugs, crime, and vice in the most crowded tenement areas, where walls and sidewalks are covered with spray-painted phone numbers. Some are for prostitutes, but many are for vendors who can provide fake documents—health certificates, diplomas, residence credentials—for those seeking work.

The Sheraton Four Points is part of the process that keeps Shenzhen growing. It is one of the places foreigners go when they are ready to buy from China.

The foreigners in their thirties through fifties who come to Shanghai are often financiers, consultants, or lawyers. They tend to be lean, with good suits and haircuts. Those in Beijing are often diplomats or academics, or they're from foundations or NGOs. They look a little less polished. The scene in and around Shenzhen is different. It is an international group—Americans, Taiwanese, Europeans, Japanese—of a single class. Virtually all of them are designers, engineers, or buyers from foreign companies who have come to meet with Chinese factory owners. The Americans in the group tend to be beefier than the Shanghai-Beijing crowd, and more Midwestern-looking. Some wear company shirts or nylon jackets with their company's logo on the pocket.

When the Four Points restaurant opens at 6:30 in the morning, foreigners begin assembling for breakfast, the meal when people most crave their native cuisine. It is laid out for all comers on a huge buffet: for the Europeans, sliced meats and cheese, good breads, strong coffee, muesli and yogurt. For the Japanese, pickles, sushi, cold noodles, smoked eel over rice. For the Taiwanese and other Chinese, steamed buns, dim sum, hot congee cereal. For the Americans, the makings of a Denny's-style "Slam" breakfast: thick waffles, eggs, hash brown potatoes, sausage and bacon and ham. My wife finally accused me of spending so much time in Shenzhen just for the breakfasts.

The room is noisy, as people discuss their plans for the day or meet the Chinese factory officials who will conduct them on their tours. The room empties dramatically by nine o'clock, as people go out to meet their drivers and vans, and the day's factory touring and contract signing begin. As best I could tell from chatting with fellow guests, in all my trips to the Four Points, I was the only person there not on a buying mission.

Nearly every morning one man, a forty-one-year-old Irish bachelor, sits at the same table at the Four Points. Very late in the evening, he is at that table for dinner, too. The table is near the entrance, from which the rest of the room can be surveyed. On a typical night, the company he owns will have ten to fifteen rooms booked at the hotel for foreign visitors coming to do business with him. Often a few will join him for dinner. When the waiters see this man coming, they bring the plain Western food—meat, potatoes—they know he's interested in. "Do you have the same thing every night?" I asked him when I saw the waiters' reflexive response to his arrival. "I didn't come here for the food," he replied.

This man has lived in an apartment at the Four Points for the last two years, and in other hotels around Shenzhen for the previous eight. He makes a point of telling people that he does not speak Chinese—most business visitors who try, he says, have to work so hard to cope with the language that they forget what they're negotiating about. But at useful points in meetings he drops in Chinese colloquialisms so that people must wonder whether in fact he has understood everything that has been said. (He tells me he hasn't.) His name is Liam Casey, and I have come to think of him as "Mr. China."

"Mr. China" is an established jokey honorific, like *People* magazine's "Sexiest Man Alive—2003." Since the days of Marco Polo, successive foreigners have competed informally for recognition as the person who *really* understands the country and can make things happen here. The hilarious 2005 memoir *Mr. China*, by Tim Clissold, describes the heartbreak and frustration of a young British financier who thought he could figure out the secrets of success in China when it was first opening up to Western commerce.

Liam Casey has succeeded where Tim Clissold was frustrated, but he is careful not to sound overconfident. "Just when you think you know what's happening here, that's when you're in danger," he says. "You see some new product on the market, and you wonder where it was made—and it turns out to be a factory you drove by every day for five years and never knew what was going on inside! You can be here so long and know so little." But for my purposes he is Mr. China, because he is at the center of the overlapping flows of humanity bringing the world's work to China.

When not dining or sleeping at the Four Points, Casey runs a company he owns outright, with 800 employees (50 of them are from Ireland, America, or one of a dozen other nations; the rest are Chinese) and sales in 2006 of about $125 million. He is of medium height and fit-seeming in a compact way, with thick dark hair and a long face that generally has an impish expression. He has a strong Irish accent and dresses informally. He walks, talks, and moves so fast that I am generally scrambling to keep up.

Casey grew up on a farm outside Cork, had no formal education after high school, and first worked as a salesman in garment shops in Cork and then Dublin. He got involved in buying garments from Europe, with a friend set up a Crate & Barrel–style store in Ireland, and then decided to travel. At age 29 he arrived in Southern California and worked briefly for a trading company. He says he would be in America still—"Laguna, Newport Beach, ah, I luvved it"—but he could not get a green card or long-term work permit and didn't want to try to stay there under the radar.

(I might as well say this in every article I write from overseas: The easier America makes it for talented foreigners to work and study there, the richer, more powerful, and more respected America will be. America's ability to absorb the world's talent is the crucial advantage no other culture can match—as long as America doesn't forfeit this advantage with visa rules written mainly out of fear.)

So in 1996, just after he turned 30, Casey went to Taipei for an electronics trade show. It was his first trip to Asia, and he says, "I could see this is where the opportunity was." Within a year, he had set up operations in the Shenzhen area and started the company now known as PCH China Solutions. The initials stand for Pacific Coast Highway, in honor of his happy Southern California days.

What does this company do? The short answer is outsourcing, which in effect means matching foreign companies that want to sell products with Chinese suppliers who can make those products for them. Casey describes his mission as "helping innovators leverage the manufacturing supply chain here in China." To see how this works, consider the great human flows that now converge in southern China, which companies like Casey's help mediate.

One is the enormous flow of people, mainly young and unschooled, from China's farms and villages to Shenzhen and similar cities. Some arrive with a factory job already arranged by relatives or fixers; some come to the cities and then look for work. In the movie version of *Balzac and the Little Chinese Seamstress*, two teenage men from the city befriend a young woman in the mountain village where they have been sent for rustication during the Cultural Revolution. One day the young woman unexpectedly leaves. She has gone to "try her luck in a big city," her grandfather tells them. "She said she wanted a new life." The new life is in Shenzhen.

Multiplied millions of times, and perhaps lacking the specific drama of the *Balzac* tale, this is the story of the factory towns. As in the novel, many of the migrants are young women. In the light-manufacturing operations I have seen in the Pearl River Delta and around Shanghai, the workforce is predominantly female. Signing on with a factory essentially means making your job your life. Workers who come to the big coastal factory centers either arrive, like the little seamstress, before they have a spouse or children, or leave their dependents at home with grandparents, aunts, or uncles. At the electronics and household-goods factories, including many I've seen, the pay is between 900 and 1,200 RMB per month [about $130–$175 in late 2008]. In the villages the workers left, a farm family's cash earnings might be a few thousand RMB per year. Pay is generally lowest, and discipline toughest, at factories owned and managed by Taiwanese or mainland Chinese companies. The gigantic Foxconn (run by its founder, Terry Gou of Taiwan) is known for a militaristic organization and approach. Jobs with Western firms are the cushiest but are also rare, since the big European and American companies buy mainly from local subcontractors. Casey says that monthly pay in some factories he owns is several hundred RMB more than the local average. His goal is to retain workers for longer than the standard few-year stint, allowing them to develop greater skills and a sense of company spirit.

A factory work shift is typically 12 hours, usually with two breaks for meals (subsidized or free), six or seven days per week. Whenever the action lets up—if the assembly line is down for some reason, if workers have spare time at a meal break—many people place their heads down on the table in front of them and appear to fall asleep instantly. Chinese law says that the standard workweek is 40 hours, so this means a lot of overtime, which is included in the pay rates above. Since their home villages may be several days' travel by train and bus, workers from the hinterland usually go back only once a year. They all go at the same time—during the "Spring Festival," or Chinese New Year, when ports and factories effectively close for a week or so and the nation's transport system is choked. "The people here work hard," an American manager in a U.S.-owned plant told me. "They're young. They're quick. There's none of this 'I have to go pick up the kids' nonsense you get in the States."

At every electronics factory I've seen, each person on an assembly line has a bunch of documents posted by her workstation: her photo, name, and employee number, often the instructions she is to follow in both English and Chinese. Often too there's a visible sign of how well she's doing. For the production line as a whole there are hourly totals of target and actual production, plus allowable and actual defect levels. At several Taiwanese-owned factories I've seen, the indicator of individual performance is a childish outline drawing of a tree with leaves. After each day's shift, one of the tree's leaves is filled in with a colored marker, either red or green. If the leaf is green, the worker has met her quota and caused no problems. If it's red, a defect has been traced back to her workstation. One red leaf per month is within tolerance; two is a problem.

As in all previous great waves of industrialization, many people end up staying in town; that's why Shenzhen has grown so large. But more often than was the case during

America's or England's booms in factory work, many rural people, especially the young women, work for two or three years and then go back to the country with their savings. In their village they open a shop, marry a local man and start a family, buy land, or use their earnings to help the relatives still at home.

Life in the factories is obviously hard, and in the heavy-industry works it is very dangerous. In the same week that 32 people were murdered at Virginia Tech, 32 Chinese workers at a steel plant in the north were scalded to death when a ladleful of molten steel was accidentally dumped on them. Even in Chinese papers, that story got less play than the U.S. shooting—and fatal coal-mine disasters are so common that they are reported as if they were traffic deaths. By comparison, the light industries that typify southern China are tedious but less overtly hazardous. As the foreman of a Taiwanese electronics factory put it to me when I asked him about rough working conditions, "Have you ever seen a Chinese farm?" An American industrial designer who works in China told me about a U.S. academic who toured his factory and was horrified to see young female workers chained to their stations. What she saw was actually the grounding wire that is mandatory in most electronics plants. Each person on the assembly line has a Velcro band around her wrist, which is connected to the worktable to avoid a static-electricity buildup that could destroy computer chips.

That so many people are in motion gives Shenzhen and surrounding areas a rootless, transient quality. The natural language of southern China is Cantonese, but in the factory cities the lingua franca is Mandarin, the language that people from different parts of China are likeliest to share. "I don't like it here," a Chinese manager originally from Beijing told me, three years into a work assignment to Shenzhen. "There are no roots or culture."

"For the first few weeks I was here, I thought it was soulless," Liam Casey says of the town that has been his home for 10 years. "But like any fast-moving place, the activity *is* the character. It's like New York. You arrive at the airport and go downtown, and when you get out of that cab, no one knows where you came from. You could have been there one hour, you could have been there ten years—no one can tell. It's similar here, which makes it exciting." Casey told me that, to him, Shanghai felt slow "and made for tourists." Indeed, I am regularly surprised to find that people stroll rather than stride along the sidewalks of Shanghai: It's a busy city with slow pedestrians. Or maybe Casey's outlook is contagious.

Another great flow into Shenzhen and similar cities is of entrepreneurs who have come and set up factories. The point of the Shenzhen liberalizations was less to foster any one industry than to make it easy for businesses in general to get a start.

Many entrepreneurs attracted by the offer came from Taiwan, whose economy is characterized by small, mainly family-owned firms like those that now abound in southern China. Overall, mainland China's development model is closer to Taiwan's than to Japan's or Korea's. In all these countries and throughout East Asia, governments have used many tools to maximize industrial output: tax policy, trading rules, currency values, and so on. But Japanese and Korean policy has tended to emphasize the welfare of large, national-champion firms—Mitsubishi and Toyota, Lucky Goldstar (or LG Corp.) and Samsung—whereas Taiwan's exporters have been thousands of small firms, a few of which grew large. China is, of course, vaster than the other countries combined, but its export-oriented companies are small. One reason for the atomization is pervasive mistrust and corruption, plus a shaky rule of law. Even Foxconn, China's largest exporter, was only No. 206 on 2006's *Fortune* Global 500 list of the biggest companies in the world. When foreigners have trouble entering the Japanese or Korean markets, it is often because they run up against barriers protecting big, well-known local interests. The problem in China is typically the opposite: Foreigners don't know where to start or whom to deal with in the chaos of small, indistinguishable firms.

For me, the fragmented nature of the Chinese system is symbolized by yet another of the stunning sights in Shenzhen: the SEG Electronics Market, a seven-story downtown structure whose every inch is crammed with the sales booths of hundreds of mom-and-pop electronics dealers. "Chips that I couldn't dream of buying in the U.S., reels of rare ceramic capacitors that I only dream about at night!" Andrew "bunnie" Huang, a Chinese American electronics Ph.D. from MIT, wrote in his blog after a visit. "My senses tingle, my head spins. I can't suppress a smirk of anticipation as I walk around the next corner, to see shops stacked floor to ceiling with probably a hundred million resistors and capacitors." As he noted, "within an hour's drive north" are hundreds of factories that can "take any electronics idea and pump them out by the literal boatload." The market is part permanent trade show, part supply stop for people who suddenly need some capacitors or connectors for a prototype or last-minute project, part swap meet where traders unload surplus components.

One last flow coming into Shenzhen, which makes the other flows possible, is represented by the people at the Four Points: buyers from high-wage countries who have decided that they want to take advantage of, rather than compete with, low-cost Chinese manufacturers. This is where our Mr. China, and others like him, fit in.

This is also where a veil falls. In decades of reporting on military matters, I have rarely encountered people as concerned about keeping secrets as the buyers and suppliers who meet in Shenzhen and similar cities. What information are they committed to protect? Names, places, and product numbers that would reveal which Western companies obtain which exact products from which Chinese suppliers. There are high- and low-road reasons for their concern.

The low-road reason is the "Nike problem." This is the buyers' wish to minimize their brand's association with outsourcing in general and Asian sweatshops in particular, named for Nike's PR problems because of its factories in Indonesia. By Chinese standards, the most successful exporting factories are tough rather than abusive, but those are not the standards Western customers might apply.

The high-road reason involves the crucial operational importance of the "supply chain." It is not easy to find the right factory, work out the right manufacturing system, ensure the right supply of parts and raw material, impose the right quality standards, and develop the right relationship of trust and reliability. Companies that have solved these problems don't want to tell their competitors how they did so. "Supply chain *is* intellectual property," is the way Liam Casey puts it. Asking a Western company to specify its Chinese suppliers is like asking a reporter to hand over a list of his best sources.

Because keeping the supply chain confidential is so important to buyers, they try to impose confidentiality on their suppliers. When an outside company's reputation for design and quality is strong—Sony, Braun, Apple—many Chinese contractors like to drop hints that they are part of its supply chain. But the ones who really are part of it must be more discreet if they want to retain the buying company's trust (and business).

So I will withhold details but ask you to take this leap: If you think of major U.S. or European brand names in the following businesses, odds are their products come from factories like those I'm about to describe. The businesses are computers, including desktops, laptops, and servers; telecom equipment, from routers to mobile phones; audio equipment, including anything MP3-related, home stereo systems, most portable devices, and headsets; video equipment of all sorts, from cameras and camcorders to replay devices; personal-care items and high-end specialty catalog goods; medical devices; sporting goods and exercise equipment; any kind of electronic goods or accessories; and, for that matter, just about anything else you can think of. Some of the examples I'll give come from sites in Shenzhen, but others are from facilities near Shanghai, Hangzhou, Guangzhou, Xiamen, and elsewhere.

Why does a foreign company come to our Mr. China? I asked Casey what he would tell me if I were in, say, some branch of the steel industry in Pittsburgh and was looking to cut costs. "Not interested," he said. "The product's too heavy, and you've probably already automated the process, so one person is pushing a button. It would cost you almost as much to have someone push the button in China."

But what is of intense interest to him, he said, is a company that has built up a brand name and relationships with retailers and knows what it wants to promote and sell next—and needs to save time and money in manufacturing a product that requires a fair amount of assembly. "That is where we can help, because you will come here and see factories that are better than the ones you've been working with in America or Germany."

Here are a few examples, all based on real-world cases: You have announced a major new product that has gotten great buzz in the press. But close to release time, you discover a design problem that must be fixed—and no U.S. factory can adjust its production process in time.

The Chinese factories can respond more quickly, and not

simply because of 12-hour workdays. "Anyplace else, you'd have to import different raw materials and components," Casey told me. "Here, you've got nine different suppliers within a mile, and they can bring a sample over that afternoon. People think China is cheap, but really, it's *fast*." Moreover, the Chinese factories use more human labor, and fewer expensive robots or assembly machines, than their counterparts in rich countries. "People are the most adaptable machines," an American industrial designer who works in China told me. "Machines need to be reprogrammed. You can have people doing something entirely different next week."

Or: You are an American inventor with a product you think has "green" potential for household energy savings. But you need to get it to market fast, because you think big companies may be trying the same thing, and you need to meet a target retail price of $100. "No place but China to do this," Mr. China said, as he showed me the finished product.

Or: You are a very famous American company, and you worry that you've tied up too much capital keeping inventory for retail stores at several supply depots in America. With Mr. China's help, you start emphasizing direct retail sales on your Web site—and do all the shipping and fulfillment from one supply depot, run by young Chinese women in Shenzhen, who can ship directly to specific retail stores.

Over the course of repeated visits to Shenzhen—the breakfasts!—and visits to other manufacturing regions, I heard about many similar cases and saw some of the tools that have made it possible for Western countries to view China as their manufacturing heartland.

Some involve computerized knowledge. Casey's PCH has a Google Earth–like system that incorporates what he has learned in 10 years of dealing with Chinese subcontractors. You name a product you want to make—say, a new case or headset for a mobile phone. Casey clicks on the map and shows the companies that can produce the necessary components—and exactly how far they are from one another in travel time. This is hard-won knowledge in an area where city maps are out-of-date as soon as they are published and addresses are approximate. (Casey's are keyed in with GPS coordinates, discreetly read from his GPS-equipped mobile phone when he visits each factory.) If a factory looks promising, you click again and get interior and exterior photos, a rundown on the management, in some cases videos of the assembly line in action, plus spec sheets and engineering drawings for orders it has already filled. Similar programs allow Casey and his clients to see which ship, plane, or truck their products are on anywhere in the world, and the amount of stock on hand in any warehouse or depot. (How do they know? Each finished piece and almost every component has an individual bar code that is scanned practically every time it is touched.)

The factories whose work flow Casey monitors vary tremendously, though not in their looks. I've come to think that there is only one set of blueprints for factories in China: a big, boxy, warehouse-looking structure, usually made of concrete and usually five stories; white or gray outside; relatively large windows, which is how you can tell it from the workers' dormitories; high ceilings, to accommodate machines. But inside, some are highly automated while some are amazingly reliant on hand labor. I'm not even speaking of the bad, dangerous, and out-of-date factories frequently found in the north of China, where leftover Maoist-era heavy-industry hulks abound. Even some newly built facilities leave to human hands work that has been done in the West for many decades by machines. Imagine opening a consumer product—a mobile phone, an electric toothbrush, a wireless router—and finding a part that was snapped on or glued into place. It was probably put there by a young Chinese woman who did the same thing many times per minute throughout her 12-hour workday.

I could describe many installations, but I was fascinated by two. The first represents one extreme in automation. It is owned and operated by Inventec, one of five companies based in Taiwan that together produce the vast majority of laptop and notebook computers sold under any brand anywhere in the world. Everyone in America has heard of Dell, Sony, Compaq, HP, Lenovo-IBM ThinkPad, Apple, NEC, Gateway, Toshiba. Almost no one has heard of Quanta, Compal, Inventec, Wistron, or ASUSTeK. Yet nearly 90 percent of laptops and notebooks sold under the famous brand names are actually made by one of these five companies in their factories in mainland China. I have seen a factory with three "competing" brand names coming off the same line.

The Inventec installation I saw was in an export-processing zone in Shanghai specially created for the company, in which imported components for manufacturing and finished products for export were free of the usual duties or taxes. It turns out more than 30,000 notebook computers per day, under one of the brand names listed above. Each day, an Inventec plant on the same campus produces hundreds of large, famous-brand-name server computers to run Internet traffic.

This is today's rough counterpart to the Ford Motor Company's old River Rouge works. In the heyday of The Rouge, rubber, steel, and other raw materials would come into the plant, and finished autos would come out. Here, naked green circuit boards, capacitors, chip sets, and other components come in each day, and notebook computers come out. Some advanced components arrive already assembled: disk drives from Taiwan or Singapore, LCD screens from Korea or Japan, keyboards and power supplies from other plants in China.

The overall process looks the way you would expect a high-tech assembly line to. Conveyors and robots take the evolving computer from station to station; each unit arrives in front of a worker a split second after she has finished with the previous one. Before a component goes into a machine, its bar code is scanned to be sure it is the right part; after it is added, the machine is "check-weighed" to see that its new weight is correct. Hundreds of tiny transistors, chips, and other electronic parts are attached to each circuit board by "pick and place" robots, whose multiple arms move almost too fast to follow. The welds on the board are scanned with lasers for defects. Any with problems are set aside for women specialists, looking through huge magnifying glasses, to reweld. "Why did this factory invest so much in robots and machine tools?" I asked a supervisor from Taiwan. "People can't do it precisely enough," was his answer. These factories automate not what's too expensive but what's too delicate for human beings to perform.

Many of the notebook computers have been ordered online, and as they near completion each is "flavored" for its destination. The day I visited, one was going to Tokyo, with a Japanese keyboard installed and Japanese logos snapped into the right places on the case; the next one was headed for the United States. After display screens are installed, each computer rides on a kind of racetrack along the ceiling of the factory, where it runs for several hours to make sure that all components work. Then the conveyors carry it to the final flavoring step—the "burn in" of the operating system, which on my visit was Windows Vista, in many languages. One engineer pointed out that because Vista requires up to 10 times as much disk space as Windows XP, the assembly line had to be altered to allow a much longer, slower passage through the burn-in station.

The other facility that intrigued me, one of Liam Casey's in Shenzhen, handled online orders for a different well-known American company. I was there around dawn, which was crunch time. Because of the 12-hour time difference from the U.S. East Coast, orders Americans place in the late afternoon arrive in China in the dead of night. As I watched, a customer in Palatine, Illinois, perhaps shopping from his office, clicked on the American company's Web site to order two $25 accessories. A few seconds later, the order appeared on the screen 7,800 miles away in Shenzhen. It automatically generated a packing and address slip and several bar-coded labels. One young woman put the address label on a brown cardboard shipping box and the packing slip inside. The box moved down a conveyor belt to another woman working a "pick to light" system: She stood in front of a kind of cupboard with a separate open-fronted bin for each item customers might order from the Web site; a light turned on over each bin holding a part specified in the latest order. She picked the item out of that bin, ran it past a scanner that checked its number (and signaled the light to go off), and put it in the box. More check-weighing and rescanning followed, and when the box was sealed, young men added it to a shipping pallet.

By the time the night shift was ready to leave—8 a.m. China time, 7 p.m. in Palatine, 8 p.m. on the U.S. East Coast—the volume of orders from America was tapering off. More important, the FedEx pickup time was drawing near. At 9 a.m. couriers would arrive and rush the pallets to the Hong Kong airport. The FedEx flight to Anchorage would leave by 6 p.m., and when it got there, the goods on this company's pallets would be combined with other Chinese exports and re-sorted for destinations in America. Forty-eight hours after the man in Palatine clicked "Buy it now!" on his computer, the item showed up at his door. Its return address was a company warehouse in the United States; a small MADE IN CHINA label was on the bottom of the box.

At 8 a.m. in Shenzhen, the young women on the night shift got up from the assembly line, took off the hats and hairnets they had been wearing, and shook out their dark hair. They passed through the metal detector at the door to their workroom (they pass through it going in and coming out) and walked downstairs to the racks where they had left their bikes. They wore red company jackets as part of their working uniform—and, as an informal uniform, virtually every one wore tight, low-rise blue jeans with embroidery or sequins on the seams. Most of them rode their bikes back to the dormitory; others walked, or walked their bikes, chatting with one another. That evening they would be back at work. Meanwhile, flocks of red-topped, blue-bottomed young women on the day shift filled the road, riding their bikes in.

GOOD FOR US—FOR NOW

What should we make of this? The evidence suggests what I hadn't expected: that the interaction has been good for most participants—so far.

Has the factory boom been good for China? Of course it has. Yes, it creates environmental pressures that, if not controlled, could pollute China and the world out of existence. The national government's current Five-Year Plan—the 11th, running through 2010—has as its central theme China's development as a "harmonious society," or *hexie shehui*, a phrase heard about as often from China's leadership as "global war on terror" has been heard from America's. In China, the phrase is code for attempting to deal with income inequalities, especially the hardships of farmers and millions of migrant laborers. But it is also code for at least talking about protecting the environment.

And, yes, throughout China's boom many people have been mistreated, oppressed, sometimes worked to death in factories. Even those not abused may be lonely and lost, with damaging effects on the country's social fabric. But this was also the story of Britain and America when they built their great industries, their great turbulent industrial cities, and ultimately their great industrial middle classes. For China, it is far from the worst social disruption the country has endured in the last 50 years. At least this upheaval, unlike the disastrous Great Leap Forward of the 1950s and Cultural Revolution of the 1960s and early 1970s, has some benefits for individuals and the nation.

Some Westerners may feel that even today's "normal" Chinese working conditions amount to slave labor—perhaps $225 a month, no life outside the factory, work shifts so long there's barely time to do more than try to sleep in a jam-packed dormitory. Here is an uncomfortable truth I'm waiting for some Chinese official to point out: The woman from the hinterland working in Shenzhen is arguably better off economically than an American in Chicago living on minimum wage. She can save most of what she makes and feel she is on the way up; the American can't and doesn't. Over the next two years, the minimum wage in the United States is expected to rise to $7.25 an hour. Assuming a 40-hour week, that's just under $1,200 per month, or about 5 times the Chinese factory wage. But that's before payroll deductions and the cost of food and housing, which are free or subsidized in China's factory towns.

Chinese spokesmen do make a different point about their economy, and they rattle it off so frequently that Western audiences are tempted to dismiss it. They say, "Whatever else we have done, we have brought hundreds of millions of people out of poverty." That is true, it is important, and the manufacturing export boom has been a significant part of how China has done it. This economic success obviously does not justify everything the regime has done, especially its crushing of any challenge to one-party rule. But the magnitude of the achievement can't be ignored. For all of the billions of dollars given in foreign aid and supervised by the World Bank, the greatest good for the greatest number of the world's previously impoverished people in at least the last half century has been achieved in China, thanks largely to the outsourcing boom.

Has the move to China been good for American companies? The answer would seemingly have to be yes—otherwise, why would they go there? It is conceivable that bad partnerships, stolen intellectual property, dilution of brand name, logistics nightmares, or other difficulties have given many companies a sour view of outsourcing; I have heard examples in each category from foreign executives. But the more interesting theme I have heard from them, which explains why they are willing to surmount the inconveniences, involves something called the "smiley curve."

The curve is named for the U-shaped arc of the 1970s-era smiley-face icon, and it runs from the beginning to the end of a product's creation and sale. At the beginning is the company's brand: HP, Siemens, Dell, Nokia, Apple. Next comes the idea for the product: an iPod, a new computer, a camera phone. After that is high-level industrial design—the conceiving of how the product will look and work. Then the detailed engineering design for how it will be made. Then the necessary components. Then the actual manufacture and assembly. Then the shipping and distribution. Then retail sales. And finally, service contracts and sales of parts and accessories.

The significance is that China's activity is in the middle stages—manufacturing, plus some component supply and engineering design—but America's is at the two ends, and those are where the money is. The smiley curve, which shows the profitability or value added at each stage, starts high for branding and product concept, swoops down for manufacturing, and rises again in the retail and servicing stages. The simple way to put this—that the real money is in brand name, plus retail—may sound obvious, but its implications are illuminating.

At each factory I visited, I asked managers to estimate how much of a product's sales price ended up in whose hands. The strength of the brand name was the most important variable. If a product is unusual enough and its brand name attractive enough, it could command so high a price that the retailer might keep half the revenue. (Think an Armani suit, a Starbucks latte.) Most electronics products are now subject to much fiercer price competition, since it is so easy for shoppers to find bargains on the Internet. Therefore the generic Windows-style laptops I saw in one modern factory might go for around $1,000 in the United States, with the retailer keeping less than $50.

Where does the rest of the money go? The manager of that factory guessed that Intel and Microsoft together would collect about $300, and that the makers of the display screen, the disk-storage devices, and other electronic components might get $150 or so apiece. The keyboard makers would get $15 or $20; FedEx or UPS would get slightly less. When all other costs were accounted for, perhaps $30 to $40—3 to 4 percent of the total—would stay in China with the factory owners and the young women on the assembly lines.

Other examples: A carrying case for an audio device from a big-name Western company retails for just under $30. That company pays the Chinese supplier $6 per case, of which about half goes for materials. The other $24 stays with the big-name company. An earphone-like accessory for another U.S.-brand audio device also retails for about $30. Of this, I was told, $3 stays in China. I saw a set of high-end Ethernet connecting cables. The cables are sold, with identical specifications but in three different kinds of packaging, in three forms in the United States: as a specialty product, as a house brand in a nationwide office-supply store, and with no brand over eBay. The retail prices are $29.95 for the specialty brand, $19.95 in the chain store, and $15.95 on eBay. The Shenzhen-area company that makes them gets $2 apiece.

In case the point isn't clear: Chinese workers making a few hundred dollars a month have been helping American designers, marketers, engineers, and retailers who make larger amounts each week earn even more. Plus, they have helped shareholders of U.S.-based companies.

All this is apart from a phenomenon that will be the subject of a future article: China's conversion of its trade surpluses into a vast hoard of dollar-denominated reserves. Everyone understands that in the short run China's handling of its reserves has been a convenience to the United States. By placing more than $1 trillion in U.S. stock and bond markets, it has propped up the U.S. economy. Asset prices are higher than they would otherwise be; interest rates are lower, whether for American families taking out mortgages or for American taxpayers financing the ever-mounting federal debt. The dollar has also fallen less than it otherwise would have—which in the short run helps American consumers keep buying Chinese goods.

Everyone also understands that in the long run China must change this policy. Its own people need too many things— schools, hospitals, railroads—for it to keep sending its profits to America. It won't forever sink its savings into a currency, the dollar, virtually guaranteed to keep falling against the RMB. This year the central government created a commission to consider the right long-term use for China's reserves. No one expects the recommendation to be: Keep buying dollars. How and when the change will occur, what it will be, and what consequences it will have, is what everyone would like to know.

One other aspect of China's development to date has helped American companies in their dealings with it. This is the fact that China, so far, has been different in crucial ways from America's previous great Asian challenger: Japan. Americans have come to view the Japanese economy as a kind of joke, mainly because the Tokyo Stock Exchange has been in a slump for nearly 20 years. Nonetheless, Japan remains the world's second-largest economy. Toyota has overtaken General Motors to become the largest automaker; Japan's exporters have continually increased their sales of electronics and other high-value goods; and the long-standing logic of the Japanese system, in which consumers and investors suffer so that producers may thrive, remains intact.

Japan was already a rich and modern country, as China still is not, by the time trade friction intensified in the 1980s. More important, its leading companies were often competing head-to-head with established high-value, high-tech companies in the United States: Fujitsu against IBM, Toshiba against Intel, Fuji against Kodak, Sony and Matsushita against Motorola, and on down the list. Gains for Japanese companies often meant direct losses for companies in America—whether those companies were seen as stodgy and noninnovative, like the Detroit firms, or technologically agile and advanced, like the semiconductor makers.

For the moment, China's situation is different. Its companies are numerous but small. Lenovo and Tsingtao are its two globally recognized brand names. But Lenovo is known mainly because it bought the ThinkPad brand from IBM, and a quarter of Tsingtao Beer is owned by Anheuser-Busch. Chinese exporters have done best when working for, rather than against, Western companies, as Foxconn (like numerous smaller firms) has in working with Apple. While the Chinese government obviously wants to strengthen the country's brands—for instance, with an aircraft company it hopes will compete with Boeing and Airbus—its "industrial planning" has mainly taken the form not of specific targeting but of general business promotion, as with the incentives that brought companies to Shenzhen.

China's economy, technically still socialist, has also been

strangely more open than Japan's. Through its first four decades of growth after World War II, Japan was essentially closed to foreign ownership and investment. (Texas Instruments and IBM were two highly publicized exceptions to the rule.) China's industrial boom, by contrast, is occurring during the age of the World Trade Organization, to which it was admitted in 2001. Under WTO rules, China is obliged to open itself to foreign investment and ownership at a much earlier stage of its development than Japan did. Its export boom has been led by foreign firms. China is rife with intellectual piracy, hidden trade barriers, and other impediments. But overall it is harder for foreign economies or foreign companies to claim damage from China's trade policies than from Japan's.

When I was living in Japan through its boom of the late 1980s, I argued that its behavior illustrated some great historic truths that economic models cannot easily include. Sometimes societies pursue goals other than the one economists consider rational: the greatest possible growth of consumer well-being. This has been true of America, mainly during wartime but also when it has pursued martial-toned projects thought to be in the nation's interest: building interstate highways, sending men into space, perhaps someday developing alternative energy supplies. In a more consistent way, over decades, this has been true of Japan.

For anyone who has taken Econ 101, the natural response would be: That's their problem! They're making high-quality products for everyone else, so what's not to like? But in the past decade, a growing number of respectable economists have argued that the situation is not that simple. If one nation deliberately promotes high-tech and high-value industries, it can end up with more of those industries, and more of the high-wage jobs that go with them, than it would have otherwise. This is not economically "rational"—European countries have paid heavily for each job they have created through Airbus. But Boeing sells fewer airplanes and employs fewer engineers than it presumably would without competition from Airbus. The United States does not have to emulate Europe's approach, or Japan's. But it needs to be aware of them, and of the possible consequences. (With different emphases, Paul Samuelson of MIT, Alan Blinder and William Baumol of Princeton, and Ralph Gomory, head of the Alfred P. Sloan Foundation, have advanced this argument.)

China's behavior, and that of its companies, is easier to match with standard economic theories than Japan's. So far, deals like those struck at the Sheraton Four Points have been mainly good for all parties. Chinese families have new opportunities in life. American customers have wider choices. American investors have better returns. But, of course, there are complications.

First is the social effect visible around the world, which in homage to China's Communist past we can call "intensifying the contradictions." Global trade involves one great contradiction: The lower the barriers to the flow of money, products, and ideas, the less it matters where people live. But because most people cannot move from one country to another, it will always matter where people live. In a world of frictionless, completely globalized trade, people on average would all be richer—but every society would include a wider range of class, comfort, and well-being than it now does. Those with the most marketable global talents would be richer, because they could sell to the largest possible market. Everyone else would be poorer, because of competition from a billions-strong labor pool. With no trade barriers, there would be no reason why the average person in, say, Holland would be better off than the average one in India. Each society would contain a cross section of the world's whole income distribution—yet its people would have to live within the same national borders.

We're nowhere near that point. But the increasing integration of the American and Chinese economies pushes both countries toward it. This is more or less good for China, but not all good for America. It means economic benefits mainly for those who have already succeeded, a harder path up for those who are already at a disadvantage, and further strain on the already weakened sense of fellow feeling and shared opportunity that allows a society as diverse and unequal as America's to cohere.

A further problem is that China's business and governmental leaders are all too aware of how the smiley curve affects them. Yes, it's better to have jobs that pay a few hundred dollars a month than none at all. But it would be better still to have jobs that pay many times as much and are at more desirable positions along the curve. If the United States were in China's position, it would be doing everything possible to bring more high-value work within its borders—and that, of course, is what China is trying to do. Everywhere you turn you see an illustration.

Just a few: In the far north of China, Intel has just agreed to build a major chip-fabrication plant, with high-end engineering and design jobs, not just seats on the assembly line. In Beijing, both Microsoft and Google have opened genuine research centers, not just offices to serve the local market. Down in Shenzhen, Liam Casey's company is creating industrial-design centers, where products will be conceived, not just snapped together. What was recently a factory zone in Shanghai is being gentrified; local authorities are pushing factories to relocate 10 miles away, so their buildings can be turned into white-collar engineering and design centers.

At the moment, most jobs I've seen the young women in the factories perform have not been "taken" from America, because in America these assembly-type tasks would be done by machines. But the Chinese goal is, of course, to build toward something more lucrative.

Many people I have spoken with say that the climb will be slow for Chinese industries, because they have so far to go in bringing their design, management, and branding efforts up to world standards. "Think about it—global companies are full of CEOs and executives from India, but very few Chinese," Dominic Barton, the chairman of McKinsey's Asia Pacific practice, told me. The main reason, he said, is China's limited pool of executives with adequate foreign-language skills and experience working abroad. Andy Switky, the managing director of Asia Pacific for the famed California design firm IDEO, described a frequent Chinese outlook toward quality control as "happy with crappy." This makes it hard for them to move beyond the local, low-value market. "Even now in China, most people don't have an iPod or a notebook computer," the manager of a Taiwanese-owned audio-device factory told me. "So it's harder for them to think up improvements, or even tell a good one from a bad one." These and other factors may slow China's progress. But that's a feeble basis for American hopes.

The measures Americans most often discuss for dealing with China are not much better as a long-term basis for hope. Yes, the RMB is now undervalued against the dollar. Yes, that makes Chinese exports cheaper than they would otherwise be. And yes, the RMB's value should rise—and it will. But at no conceivable level would it bring those Shenzhen jobs back to Ohio. At best it would make U.S. exports, from locomotives and high-tech medical equipment to wine and software, more attractive. Such commercial victories are important, but they are unlikely to be advanced by threats of retaliatory tariffs if China does not speed the RMB's climb. Also, the faster the dollar falls against the RMB, the faster Chinese authorities might move their assets out of dollars to stronger currencies.

In 2007 the U.S. government imposed special tariffs, called countervailing duties, on imports of glossy paper from China. This is the kind of paper used to print magazines and catalogs, and Chinese exports of it to the United States rose tenfold from 2004 to 2006. The U.S. government said the duties were necessary to offset the export subsidies Chinese manufacturers receive via low-cost loans, tax breaks, and other benefits. Under WTO rules, export subsidies of all sorts are prohibited; U.S. officials, academics, and trade groups have prepared lists of de facto subsidies that cut the price of Chinese goods to U.S. consumers by 25 percent, 40 percent, and even more. (The Chinese—like the Europeans, Australians, and others— are quick to retort that the United States subsidizes many products, too, especially exports from large-scale farms.)

This is obviously significant. But think again of those Ethernet connectors that retail for $29.95 and cost only $2 to make. Removing all imaginable subsidies might push the manufacturing cost to $3. Suppose it went to $4. That would have a big effect on decisions made by corporations that outsource to China. Can they raise the retail price? Must they just accept a lower margin? Should they build the next factory in Vietnam? But it would not make anyone bring production back to the United States.

Government policy and favoritism may play a big role in China's huge road-building and land-development policies, but they seem to be secondary factors in the outsourcing boom. For instance, when I asked Mr. China which officials I should try to interview in the local Shenzhen government to understand how they worked with companies, he said he didn't know. He'd never met any.

American complaints about the RMB, about subsidies, and about other Chinese practices have this in common: They assume that the solution to long-term tensions in the trading relationship lies in changes on China's side. I think that assumption is naive. If the United States is unhappy with the effects of its interaction with China, that's America's problem, not China's. To imagine that the United States can stop China from pursuing its own economic ambitions through nagging, threats, or enticement is to fool ourselves. If a country does not like the terms of its business dealings with the world, it needs to change its own policies, not expect the world to change. China has done just that, to its own benefit—and, up until now, to America's.

Are we uncomfortable with the America that is being shaped by global economic forces? The inequality? The sense of entitlement for some? Of stifled opportunity for others? The widespread fear that today's trends—borrowing, consuming, looking inward, using up infrastructure—will make it hard to stay ahead tomorrow, particularly in regard to China? If so, those trends themselves, and the American choices behind them, are what Americans can address. They're not China's problem, and they're not the fault of anyone in Shenzhen.

MACAU'S BIG GAMBLE

SEPTEMBER 2007

Today's boom times in China are interesting in their own right, as economic booms always are. By chance and by design, I have lived in the middle of several of them: the Texas oil boom of the mid-1970s, Japan's all-around boom of the late 1980s, and the Seattle and Bay Area Internet bubble of the late 1990s. Inside the boom zone, people don't spend much time thinking about how the good times began, or asking how long the boom can last. Everyone, everywhere, takes his own prosperity as a sign of cleverness, wise planning, and hard work. From outside, the questions concern the boom's effects—on culture, on values, on old establishments and traditions. Such questions about China's boom are unusually compelling, simply because of the country's scale. What will its growth mean for the global environment? For jobs and prices outside of China? For the military balance of power and the ideological contest of ideas?

Right now the very most booming part of generally booming China raises questions like these in a peculiar and intriguing form. This part is the tiny peninsula of Macau—as it spells its name, versus Macao in American usage. Geographically, it is one-sixth the size of the District of Columbia, and it has a population of half a million. It officially became Chinese territory only in 1999, after centuries of colonial control by Portugal. Like its neighbor Hong Kong, which was transferred from British to Chinese control in 1997, Macau is a "special administrative region" of China, meaning it is supposed to run by its own laws and customs for at least 50 years after the handover.

While China's overall economy has grown about 10 percent per year since the 1980s, Macau's has recently been growing by 20. While Shanghai, Beijing, and other big cities are dotted with construction cranes, Macau appears to be made of them. Early this year, on a tour of Macau's Cotai Strip, where a version of the Las Vegas Strip is being created, I counted more than 200 working cranes before I lost track. While the rest of China is struggling to contain the tensions between the very rich and the very poor, via what the central government calls its "harmonious society" policy, Macau is rushing to make itself more attractive to the very rich—and to anyone else who would like to visit the only part of Chinese territory where casino gambling is legal. (State-run lotteries are the only legal gambling outlet on the mainland.)

Last year Macau finally overtook Las Vegas in gambling revenues: Macau had about $7 billion, versus $6.5 billion for Las Vegas. As we will see, this statistical achievement is less significant than it sounds. But news outlets naturally presented it to Americans as more evidence of China's incomprehensible scale and its unstoppable rise—plus, on the bright side, as another example of the riches open to Western companies (in this case, U.S. casino firms) that can figure out how to get part of the pot-o'-gold Chinese market.

Yes, what is happening in Macau should be of intense interest to casino operators everywhere, and to the financiers and suppliers who thrive off the world's gambling industry, and to those compiling information on how Chinese people use their new wealth. But in repeated visits to Macau, I found it far more interesting than I would have guessed from most of the gambling-boom stories.

It is interesting in a lowbrow way because of Macau's ineradicable seediness. Look in one direction, and you see a new five-star hotel. Turn 90 degrees, and you see an alley down which Indiana Jones might run, pursued by gangsters, or where Sydney Greenstreet might totter out from a smoky den. But this same small locale is also deeply interesting in highbrow ways. The fate of modern Macau will be determined in part by the same political and ideological struggles that are determining so many other aspects of China's rise. The more China influences businesses and societies elsewhere, the more it comes under pressure to adhere to broadly accepted international standards rather than to its accustomed ways. These standards include such vague-sounding principles as rule of law, transparency, and accountability, which in practice mean: Can you trust a contract? Can you win a lawsuit? Do you know who's really making a decision? Will the decision be made in favor of whoever provides a "red envelope" containing the biggest bribe? How many sets of books should a company be keeping, anyway? How much money laundering is too much, if Macau wants to be internationally respectable?

Our story begins 450 years ago, when the Portuguese established effective control over Macau and began using it as their trading base for markets in China and Japan. By the mid-1800s, this business had been eclipsed by the rise of British banks and trading companies in Hong Kong. The Portuguese government of Macau responded by legalizing gambling and developing what two academic analysts recently called a "sordid" economic structure—a "mixture of gambling, opium, and coolies trade, together with prostitution, crime and contraband." The businesses reinforced one another, since peasants who fell into debt at the gambling tables or in the opium dens could be turned into coolies or indentured seamen until they worked off what they owed.

Through the world wars of the twentieth century and the rise of the Communists on the Chinese mainland, the Portuguese government oversaw Macau's casinos and its vice-based economy. The prelude to Macau's modern era began in 1962, when Stanley Ho, a 41-year-old entrepreneur from Hong Kong with a Chinese father and a Portuguese mother, paid Portugal about half a million U.S. dollars to take over monopoly rights to run all casinos in Macau. Soon he also dominated the helicopter and ferry businesses that brought customers from Hong Kong, and owned the biggest department store, the racetrack, and so on. He held a one-third share in the airport and a one-seventh share in Air Macau.

Perhaps it's not surprising to hear that now, in his mid-eighties, Ho is the richest man in Macau and one of the richest in all of China, with assets estimated at $7 billion. Or that he is debonair and sharply dressed, renowned for his skill at the tango and other ballroom dances, or that he has had, by most reports, four wives and 17 children. His flagship operation has been the Casino Lisboa—rendered in Chinese as *Pujing*, or "capital of Portugal"—which has a 1950s–Las Vegas look. (Earlier this year, he opened the glitzier, bigger Grand Lisboa Casino.) He is referred to in Macau as "Dr. Stanley Ho," including on the avenue of that name running through the middle of the town and, for a while, on his apparently now-defunct online gambling site, DrHo.com.

Stanley Ho has not been charged with any crime but is typically described (outside his home territory) as being "associated with" or "suspected of ties to" criminal gangs from Macau and surrounding areas. The New Jersey Casino Control Commission is now considering whether one of its licensees, MGM Mirage, can enter a partnership with one of Ho's daughters, Pansy Ho. The decision will turn on whether Pansy Ho, whose reputation is otherwise positive, can prove that she is wholly independent of her father's influence. (The Nevada Gaming Commission and Mississippi Gaming Commission have already considered the same question and given Pansy Ho their OK.)

By all accounts, the Macau of Stanley Ho's heyday was loose, easy, and lightly regulated. British Hong Kong attracted business through rule-of-law government and investments in infrastructure and education. Portuguese Macau enticed visitors. During the mid-1980s, my family visited Hong Kong. One day while I stayed there for meetings, my wife took our two school-age sons to Macau by ferry for a day trip. She returned ashen; they were wide-eyed after their brief visit to Gomorrah. In those days, according to a recent *Time* magazine report on the "sleazy, sleepy" city, "its architecturally charming but run-down streets were lined with hookers and occasionally reverberated with gunfire and car bombings from triad gang battles."

It's less violent now, but the old Macau is with us still. One hotel where my wife and I stayed this year doubled as a brothel featuring Russian women. On my latest visit, I stayed in Ho's original Hotel Lisboa, where the young women patrolling the corridors and popping into elevators to greet unaccompanied men were Chinese. To be fair, the city also has beautiful gardens, an informative city-history museum, a good collection of local art, elegant colonial buildings, abundant Portuguese-Chinese *estabelecimento comidas* for informal outdoor dining, and many other elements of the tropical good life. A 1,000-foot tower offers visitors a sweeping panorama of the Pearl River Delta. Sleaziness and all, it's an interesting place.

The next big change for Macau began in 1999, with the handover to China and the selection by the Chinese government of Edmund Ho (no relation to Stanley) as Macau's chief executive. This Ho was raised in Macau, educated in Canada, and worked in the United States and elsewhere before returning home in 1983, when he was in his late twenties. He participated in the negotiations for Macau's handover to China. His selection, at age 44, was seen as a significant signal that the Chinese authorities were interested in good government.

Edmund Ho quickly went to work as a reformer. "The Mafia-style murders just ceased," says William Overholt of the RAND Corporation, who lived in Hong Kong at the time. "Suddenly there was serious planning for economic development, serious investment in infrastructure, serious interest in sound business regulation." Edmund Ho apparently believed in good government, and his sponsors in Beijing thought Macau would do best if it were seriously cleaned up. In 2002, he ushered in Macau's modern age by ending Stanley Ho's monopoly and opening the casino business to foreign competitors. He acted as if he understood that the best chance to clean up the casinos would be to bring in companies that answered to laws and regulations outside Macau. At first, the rules authorized three casino operators, counting Stanley Ho (through his SJM, for Sociedade de Jogos de Macau, or "Macau Gaming Society"). Now the rules allow six.

In 2004, the first big foreign casino opened, the Sands Macao, owned by Sheldon Adelson's Las Vegas Sands company. It was an instant success, creating profits so fast that it repaid all its capital costs in less than a year. In 2006, Steve Wynn opened the Wynn Macau, with rooms much bigger, fancier, and costlier than the norm for Macau. The other competitors are Galaxy, a company founded by Hong Kong construction tycoons and based in Macau, and two foreign-based firms affiliated with Stanley Ho's children: MGM Mirage, in a 50-50 partnership with Pansy Ho, and Melco

PBL, a partnership between the Packer publishing empire of Australia and Lawrence Ho, Stanley's son. (Australian officials scrutinized his independence from his father's influence, as American officials have done with Pansy Ho, before they approved the partnership.) Those are the players. Here is the play—that is, the many interlocking struggles in Macau that together create its larger political meaning.

If you were a financial analyst, as many, many of the people I've interviewed on this subject are, you would be interested mainly in comparing the six companies' market strategies. For instance: Galaxy wants to be seen as the most authentically Chinese and is emphasizing the profitable if inelegant "grind" market.

(A note here on three terms: *gaming*, *win*, and *grind*. You can spot people who work in the gambling industry, because they always call their business "gaming." They use *gambling* only in pejorative contexts, as in "problem gambling." *Win* is the industry's term for casino profit. Financial reports from the big casino companies list "win per table," which means the house's daily take from a baccarat or roulette table. *Grind* is a business term for low-stakes, high-volume customers—in American terms, busloads of quarter-slot players headed to Atlantic City. I am looking at a report from a major U.S. bank with a section headed: "The Grind Market: Brighter Prospects.")

Galaxy's new StarWorld is set slightly askew from the main boulevard that runs in front of it. This is one signal that it's through-and-through Chinese. "Westerners look at it and say, 'It's crooked!'" Peter Caveny, head of investor relations for Galaxy, told me. "The instant Chinese look at it, they think, 'Feng shui.'" The casino has an apparently limitless supply of six-foot-tall female Chinese models who stand just inside the front door. "People come in, they see the girls, they take a picture—and go upstairs and gamble," Caveny said. "The noise, the excitement—it's all just right."

The Wynn properties take the opposite approach: classiness, modern Vegas variety. "Every one of the songs was chosen personally by Mr. Wynn," a Wynn official named Reddy Leong told me as we watched "Performance Lake" outside the hotel, which sends off fireballs and jets of water in time with music ranging from "Luck Be a Lady" to "Thus Spoke Zarathustra." The suites have high-thread-count linens, granite-appointed bathrooms bigger than my apartment in Shanghai, massage rooms with professional massage tables.

Stanley Hó's SJM is opening the most new casinos and attractions—one that looks like a temple of Babylon, one like a Tang-era Chinese fortress, one like a volcano blended with a Tibetan palace, one like a Roman amphitheater. Its biggest casino, the Grand Lisboa, is so garish I do not know where a description would begin. (Perhaps with the casino dome itself, sort of like a billion-carat faceted diamond in pink and gold, surrounded by dozens of gold-colored St. Louis–style arches.) The company will also soon open a "Prague Harbour View" hotel, presumably inspired by Prague's famous harbor.

The other competitors have varying strategies. Financial analysts are basically high on all six of the licensed casino companies.

If you were a gaming-industry insider, you would be interested in Macau mainly as the latest arena for the primeval struggle between Sheldon Adelson and Steve Wynn. In Las Vegas, the two are seen as opposite in all ways. Adelson, in his mid-seventies, is still brash and impolite, a relative newcomer to the business (he first made money with trade shows) who transformed the Las Vegas economy through his "MICE" strategy (Adelson's term for bringing customers to Las Vegas not just for gambling but for "Meetings, Incentive, Convention, and Exhibition"). Thanks largely to him, Las Vegas has changed from a weekend destination to one in which hotels are busy all week long. "I can tell you that when Sheldon Adelson decided to build the [enormous] Las Vegas Venetian and cater to conventioneers, many people thought he was crazy," Andrew Zarnett, a managing director at Deutsche Bank, said at G2E Asia, the Global Gaming Expo held in Macau. "But he was daring, he had a view, and he was right."

Unlike Adelson, who shaped Las Vegas through mass marketing, Steve Wynn, now in his mid-sixties, shaped it through high-end innovations. At industry meetings, I listened to financiers and casino veterans contrast Wynn's suaveness and perfectionism with Adelson's bluntness and commoditization. I came away thinking that Wynn's demeanor could have been the model for Wayne Newton's performance in National Lampoon's *Vegas Vacation*. "Steve Wynn was equally daring in going upscale, offering luxury and high-end restaurants, in the faith that the customer will pay," said Zarnett.

The broadening of Las Vegas's economic base is why Macau has in no sense overtaken it. Casino earnings make up nearly all of Macau's tourist-related revenue, while they're barely 40 percent of the Las Vegas Strip. The rest comes from conventions, shows, high-end dining, and fancy malls. Because of all these attractions, the average visitor to Las Vegas stays for nearly four days. The norm in Macau is still the casino-centric day trip. That's one reason Las Vegas has 130,000 hotel rooms, versus 13,000 for Macau. In size, glitziness, and overall excitement, Macau feels much more like Atlantic City—really, like an especially large concentration of Indian casinos in California—than Las Vegas. The current growth surge in Macau is meant to correct these weaknesses.

Adelson's Sands Macao is the town's biggest casino, and his 3,000-room Venetian Macao is the city's biggest hotel (plus casino and convention center). On my first visit to the Sands in January 2007, I looked from an inner balcony onto a gambling floor that, I was told, contained 20,000 customers, virtually all of whom appeared to be Chinese. The Wynn Macau looks different from anything around it: The city is aglare in blinking neon, but the only ornamentation on Wynn's hotel is a large cursive signature of his last name. The casino itself is understated, along the lines of a gentlemen's club. Hotel rooms at the Wynn are more expensive than at any major competitor, but the hotel has an 85 percent occupancy rate, versus 70 percent for Macau as a whole. In the battle for Macau, both men have won.

If you were an economist, you might be interested in Macau's test of the hypothesis that everyone who gets into the casino business wins, not just the industry's Men of Vision, like Adelson and Wynn. This is "win" in the casino sense, of course—that is, they end up with the money the customers lose.

The gambling business is unusual because of what analysts call its "supply driven" nature: The more places and ways there are to bet money, the more money people will bet. In many businesses, success for a new competitor means a defeat for those already there. In minor ways, this appears to be true even in Macau. Stanley Ho does not enjoy the monopoly he did a decade ago; as casinos add new tables, the win per table overall goes down. Some financiers worry that in the short term Macau may be adding too many gambling sites too fast.

But in the largest sense, the pie of gambling revenue grows and grows, so there's more for all. Macau's gambling win is bigger than that of Las Vegas—and Las Vegas is now adding capacity faster than it ever has before. (Macau also imposes a tax of up to 40 percent on casino earnings, far higher than in most U.S. states.) Fifty years ago, no U.S. state had a lottery; now 42 states do. "People would always ask, 'Will Atlantic City hurt Vegas?'" Zarnett said to me. "'What about Indian gaming? Or the riverboats?' They all came, and Las Vegas continued to grow. Macau won't hurt. Nothing hurts. New supply is always absorbed."

Some animals, given all the food they want, will eat practically until they burst; others eat only until they reach a certain size. I asked I. Nelson Rose, a professor at Whittier Law School who has written many books about the industry, whether any society offered evidence that at some point people would have spent "enough" on gambling. He said that specific areas, including Macau, could become over-casinoed, but that a sustained worldwide surge in demand for gambling seems to be under way. And even if there is a theoretical limit, for now the potential in Asia is limitless. The 300 million people of the United States spend about $50 billion a year on gambling. Frank Fahrenkopf, head of the American Gaming Association, points out that within a five-hour flight of Macau live more than 3 billion people, who together now spend only about $12 billion. Supply will bring demand.

If you were a gambling-equipment supplier, you would be interested in knowing whether Macau's casinos were going to make the "tables to slots" shift anytime soon. For anyone familiar with an American casino, the first glance inside the Grand Lisboa or even the Sands Macao is startling. To begin with, it's (relatively) quiet. China in general is as noisy as American casinos, but Chinese casinos are surprisingly hushed. Perhaps that's because there's practically no alcohol; attendants walk around with trays of free drinks, but the drinks are water, tea, milk, fruit juice. (The Chinese theory is that placing bets requires full concentration, and gamblers don't want to dull their senses or skills.) But mainly it's quiet because there are practically no slot machines to whoop-whoop and clunk out coins when someone wins. In Las Vegas, slots account for roughly 60 percent of the total casino win; in Macau, roughly 5 percent. Catherine Burns, vice president of marketing for the Bally slot-machine company, pointed out at the G2E conference that the total number of slots in Macau is about the same as at the Mohegan Sun in

Connecticut. What Macau's casinos have instead are "table games": not blackjack, craps, or poker—all of limited interest so far to Chinese gamblers—but roulette, a dice game called *da xiao* ("big-little"), and most of all, baccarat. Felt-covered tables for baccarat occupy most of Macau's gambling space.

Customers will be wedged six-deep around one table, while dealers stand idle at the neighboring two. This pattern arises, I was told, from the widespread belief among Chinese gamblers that there are "hot" and "cold" tables, and much of the skill in gambling involves telling them apart. (The clustering of other gamblers around a table is one clue.) This leads to the question that might interest you if you were an anthropologist—or a potential investor in Macau: Is there a distinctively Chinese attitude toward games of chance?

Nearly all customers in Macau are ethnically Chinese. They come in roughly equal shares from the mainland, Hong Kong, and Chinese communities in Southeast Asia. "Do Chinese like gambling more than other people?" asked Ivan Yiu at the conference in Macau. Yiu, himself Chinese, is the coordinator of addiction services for a group of hospitals in Hong Kong. His answer was yes. I have seen many sociological studies that support that view. Here is one of Yiu's pieces of evidence: In the United States, the overall rate of "pathological gambling" is 1.8 percent; for Chinese Americans and Chinese immigrants, it is about 3 percent. The variation, Yiu said, involves cultural characteristics and assumptions. Some of these may sound familiar to people who have seen or known problem gamblers of any background: a "lack of

probabilistic thinking," a belief that a player's skill can surmount the odds (even in baccarat and roulette, which involve
no skill beyond laying down a bet), the "delusion that one
can foresee results by intuition and control results by ritual."
The main difference, Yiu said, is that in Chinese cultures, a
larger proportion of people think this way. One other, more
distinctive factor is a traditional belief that money won in
gambling is as respectable as money earned any other way.
According to Yiu, a gambler who has a good run at the
roulette table will be just as esteemed as, say, Warren Buffett,
with allowances for difference of scale.

With the concept of respectability, we arrive at political values, regulation, and international law. If you were curious about the broad noneconomic effects of China's economic
rise, you would be watching the struggle over Macau's "VIP
rooms" as a proxy for larger questions about China's adher-
ence to "universal values."

Stanley Ho's four-decade monopoly on all casino business
might seem the strangest part of Macau's economic structure.
It was not: That distinction has belonged to the related system of VIP rooms, which has also been the foundation of
Macau's gambling economy—and which poses the greatest
challenge to Macau's ability to come into sync with international norms.

The most recent and authoritative academic study of the
topic is "VIP-Room Contractual System of Macao's Traditional Casino Industry," by William Eadington, a prominent

economist and director of the Institute for the Study of Gambling at the University of Nevada, Reno, and Wuyi Wang, of the Macao Polytechnic Institute. They write that the system arose from a quirk in Macau's location and logistics. In the 1970s, most of the customers came from Hong Kong by ferry, but there were never enough seats to satisfy demand. Scalpers moved in, buying up ferry tickets at face value and selling them for a profit. Stanley Ho believed this was bad for Macau's casinos and for the ferry, which he also owned, so he proposed a grand compromise: If the scalpers would move out of the ferry terminals, and presumably keep replacements from moving in, he would let them participate in gambling operations in special areas inside his casinos, which could be much more lucrative. Over time, the arrangement evolved into a way to increase the profits of Ho's casinos while sub-contracting much of the work of dealing with customers to a group of shady touts.

The touts' tactics varied. Sometimes, according to the professors, they would "befriend" prosperous-looking gamblers who had just gotten off the ferry from Hong Kong or had just crossed the Chinese border and lead them to casinos. It is hard to imagine visitors being this naive—"Hey, brother, looking for some action? I've got just the place!" But apparently it worked, and works, well enough to be an important part of the VIP-room business. Or junket organizers would act as travel agents, getting players to Macau and directing them to special rooms in a casino—where VIP-room contractors would extend credit to their customers and take a portion of the win. The players would have their own dealers, their own games, their own supply of food and drink, their own enter-tainment.

The win-sharing arrangements between touts, VIP-room contractors, and casinos could be quite complex. Sometimes the host casino would simply take a cut of each VIP room's action; sometimes a tout or junket operator would be paid a commission or fee. Often these independent contractors would lend money to gamblers who were running into bad luck and make their profit through the vig, or interest. Often they would be paid off through a scheme too convoluted to explain here, which involved something called a "dead chip."

Private gambling of this sort goes on everywhere—what would a Vegas movie be without a private poker game? But in Macau it was, and is, *most* of the gambling economy. Even now, some 65 percent of the money wagered in Macau is bet in VIP rooms. The rooms are not as profitable for the casinos as the grind market at its best. As Eadington and Wang explain, "VIP players may require the provision of lavish hotel rooms and high quality amenities for themselves and their entourages, expensive transportation, considerable pampering by staff, and a great deal of time and attention from senior management." But the sums wagered are so great that no Macau casino can afford not to cater to this market.

The problem with the VIP system is that while it doesn't guarantee corruption, it makes it very convenient. In theory, there's nothing wrong with private gambling areas. In practice, there has been little or no effort to check the backgrounds of the contractors. The rooms are assumed to be convenient sites for money laundering, which works this way: The Chinese government doesn't allow rich people to take their money out of the country easily, and it allows them to convert only small amounts of renminbi each year. So a factory owner from the Pearl River Delta, or a corrupt public official who has grown wealthy, will head to Macau. One Western banker with extensive experience in Macau pointed out that the city functions as one big, quasi-official money-laundering site via the numerous gold dealers' shops on either side of its border with mainland China. Chinese visitors buy gold with RMB from shops on their side of the border and then sell to dealers on the Macau side for Hong Kong dollars—a "hard" currency that can be converted into U.S. dollars or euros and sent anywhere in the world.

Something similar can go on when wealthy Chinese visit a VIP room. The room's operator lends them money for gambling—often large sums, worth thousands or millions of U.S. dollars. The loan is in Hong Kong dollars, the main betting currency of Macau (its own currency is the pataca). If the Chinese gambler wins, he now has hard currency. If he loses, he settles the debt back in China, in RMB. A related practice is "doubling down," in which the bets are made in one currency, say Hong Kong dollars, but the players agree to settle them later in another, like U.S. dollars. Exactly how the debts are paid, and just where the touts get their substantial operating capital, is obscure. But the rooms and other Macau-based services are assumed to be a major channel for money flowing illegally out of China—and North Korea.

I was able to see the VIP suites in about half the casinos I visited. In many cases, I was the only non-Chinese person on the premises, so it was hard to make an unobtrusive visit to one of the private rooms. I got into the ones I saw by asking casino management for a press tour. The rooms ranged from one seemingly as clean-cut as, say, a first-class lounge in an overseas airport (the Paiza Club, at the Sands Macao) to one at a locally owned casino I won't name, where the 20 people crowded around a baccarat table in a small room reacted to my entry as if I were a mother who had blundered into a room of teenage boys looking at skin magazines.

The VIP rooms are not the only cleanup challenge facing Macau. For instance, its banks are under pressure to tighten their rules against money laundering. This summer, the mainland government momentarily panicked Macau by making it harder for people in neighboring Guangdong province to get visas to visit Macau. (The restrictions are still in place, but the panic has ebbed. Officials in Macau now see the move not as directed against them but as part of a general effort to slow down parts of the economy that were growing unsustainably fast.) Still, the VIP-rooms issue has become central because of this conundrum: Economically, they are too important for any company to forgo, but legally, they are risky for international companies to accept.

They pose no risk to Stanley Ho's SJM, which is still the largest operator in Macau. A local reform movement would have to go to Cultural Revolution–style extremes to call his licenses into question. Galaxy, also based in Macau, is in a similar position. But Wynn, Sands, and MGM Mirage know that if they're found consorting with shady touts in Macau or laundering money from Guangzhou or Pyongyang (where

Stanley Ho has a casino), they could lose their U.S. licenses, which are vastly more valuable. Melco PBL faces a similar risk in Australia. And so it is that America's big gambling companies have been made into tribunes for good governance, transparency, the international rule of law, and a cleanup of the VIP business—mainly under pressure from the Nevada Gaming Commission and its analogues in New Jersey and Mississippi.

"In order to have any effective game, there has to be effective regulatory control," Frank Fahrenkopf said on the opening day of the gaming expo in Macau. "We have to be assured there is no money laundering. The secret to having a successful gaming industry is tough regulatory control." This is not a normal statement from the head of a trade association, but it reflects the American industry's rise toward legitimacy from the days when Bugsy Siegel helped create Las Vegas and Jimmy Hoffa's Teamsters financed its development. The state gaming commissions—which control the all-important licenses for Las Vegas, Atlantic City, and the Gulf Coast casinos of Biloxi—try to ensure these standards are met by requiring thorough checks of the backgrounds and sources of income of everyone who gets near a casino's staff. What they want to see are similar strictures in Macau for anyone operating a VIP room, as well as leakproof systems to prevent money laundering.

Fahrenkopf pointed out that over the past decade, scandals have affected the American accounting industry, banking, mutual-fund brokers, telecom companies, and many others—but not the gambling business. "This industry is licensed more carefully than any other that exists—well, I don't know about nuclear reactors," I. Nelson Rose of the Whittier Law School told me. "The Nevada application starts by asking you every address where you have *ever* lived. Every cent you have earned. Every gift you have received." This is a standard that no VIP-room tout could hope to pass, he said.

What the gaming commissions don't impose on the industry, its financiers do. The big international combines financing Macau's current expansion, from Goldman Sachs and Merrill Lynch to Deutsche Bank and Citibank, spend much of their due-diligence time vetting the casinos' provisions against money laundering to avoid what one banker called the "franchise risk" of winding up as the financiers of Chinese criminals, North Korean potentates, or other evildoers with hot cash.

So which side will prevail in the battle for Macau? The shady system that has been the backbone of its economy, and that local companies still rely on? Or the international standards that the Nevada Gaming Commission and the shareholders of the world are forcing on the likes of Wynn, Adelson, and MGM Mirage?

Fahrenkopf says that technology will again come to America's rescue: "We've got capital, but really we've got *expertise* in running a modern gaming business, which they need." Therefore, he tells me, Macanese and Chinese officials will cooperate in cleaning up the VIP system. Adam Rosenberg, a managing director and cohead of Goldman Sachs's gaming practice, says that China's interests push in the same direction, toward doing whatever will allow Macau to prosper by international standards. "China is very much a partner in the success of Macau," he says. It is also assumed to be a partner in the success of Edmund Ho, whose second term as Macau's chief executive ends in two years. Everything he does right, and every step forward Macau takes under its special-administrative-region status, reflects well on China's ability to manage its "one country, two systems" commitment.

But I. Nelson Rose says that these good intentions won't matter. "I still don't understand why Nevada approved its licensees to be associated with some of these [VIP] operators," he told me. "I think there is the potential for real disaster. Some guy will get arrested, and they'll go through his books, and it will all unravel from there."

You take your clashes of ideas where you can find them, and if you get tired of hearing about other tensions between "Chinese values" and the outside world, you can just follow the casino news out of Macau.

THE VIEW FROM THERE

NOVEMBER 2007

For 150 years, *The Atlantic* has been trying to figure out the American idea. For a quarter of that time, I've been on the job myself. The process began in earnest the first time I set foot outside the country, in the summer of 1970, when I left for graduate school in England. The real work of debating and defining a country's prospects, of course, happens inside its borders. But I've found it very useful to think about America from afar. I know it's annoying and superior-sounding to say that you see a country most clearly from the outside. (Those poor homebound hicks! They don't get the big picture the way we cosmopolites can.) But at least in one way, it's certainly true. Inside America, we discuss what the country could and should become. Outside, we see what it is—which of its traits and habits really make it unusual, the effects of what it claims to stand for, what it actually does to the rest of the world.

I am living in China now mainly to learn about China, which is similar to the reasons my wife and I have previously lived or spent extensive stretches in Ghana, Malaysia, Japan, and other places. But inevitably, we are thinking and learning about what America is. And—surprise!—we are feeling good. I am more hopeful about America and its idea than I was even 18 months ago, before coming to China.

The details of this outlook are shaped by my previous cycles of judging America from overseas, so let me explain three of the stages that led to my current, largely optimistic view. In England, I discovered that I was an American; in Japan, how essential America's ideas are to its strength; and now in China, that America's ideas are still the key to its vitality, if we don't abuse them or carelessly let them wither away.

In England in the early 1970s, I spent a lot of time grumbling with my American friends, and not just because we were spoiled. The United States was in a politically dark period then, and England's irritation with Richard Nixon or Lieutenant William Calley was often projected upon itinerant Americans. England itself was literally dark—and clammy, and cold, and threadbare. In retrospect, it's obvious that the country had not yet fully recovered from World War II. *Cool Britannia* had a different connotation than it would a generation later under Tony Blair. There was no real heating in the buildings or plumbing in the bathrooms (or novocaine in the National Health Service dental "studios"!)—points we learned to make only among ourselves, since it was a cliché among the natives that only Americans would notice.

No one could avoid noticing the near-collapse of the U.K.'s

social compact. For more than a month in 1971 we got no mail because of a postal strike, and in those days, that really mattered. The country's "dustmen," or garbage collectors, went on a prolonged strike, too. For weeks on end, electricity was available only for limited hours per day, on a rota basis. I still shiver as I remember trying to page through economics texts by the flicker from candles while clad in overcoat, scarf, and little knitted gloves with the fingertips cut off, in the 4 p.m. December twilight in a library at Oxford. I fear that the circumstances made me less respectful of the views of the English economic theorists I was reading. My wife-to-be had what we considered a wonderful job, handling rats in an experimental-psych laboratory. England's tenderhearted animal-protection laws dictated that the rat buildings, unlike the people buildings, be fully heated, so I went to see her as often as I could.

After two years of this—and, yes, wonderful adventures, and close friends from many lands, and tremendous good fortune to have had such opportunities, and a wedding in an Oxford chapel to the same rat-handling expert I am married to today (it wasn't just the heated labs), and so on—I was ready to come home, with a new understanding of what home meant.

Traits I had considered my own personal quirks, or perhaps regionalisms as a Californian, were revealed as being stereotypically American. In one way or another they involved mobility—really, class. The cheeseparing state of the British economy in those days was less disturbing, to me, than the static social concept behind it. At some point English society must have been tumultuous, open, and rapidly changing, right? That is the world Charles Dickens depicted, and the one that economic historians like David Landes said was both a source and a sign of Britain's rapid industrialization in the mid-1800s.

It did not seem that way anymore. Like any tourist, I admired the aesthetic results of a society in which people knew their place and some, in effect, served as picturesque props—the butlers polishing brass knobs, the Cockney-accented "scout" who cleaned my college room and, no joke, kept calling me "guv'nuh." At center stage were the toffs in their campy Oxford college blazers, living a life out of Waugh.

As an American, I got huffy about the idea that so many people felt born to their place, high or low, and by the very concept of "place" at all. While some of my American friends were poshing up their vowels and adopting Briticisms like "Brilliant!" or "full stop," my accent was becoming more and more ostentatiously American. The ideal I strove for was Jack Nicholson. Sure, America had its version of class mark-ers and class barriers. But they were milder and more perme-able, and Americans on the whole were embarrassed by their existence. Before coming to England, I had considered the Civil War America's most necessary struggle. As time went on, my thoughts turned admiringly to Lexington, Concord, and the Liberty Bell. America was coarser than England, but it was more independent and open, freer of class shackles. Being sure that it remained open—that as much as possible, Americans always had a second chance—took on new impor-tance to me as a cause.

Living and studying in England taught me that America meant openness. Living in Japan and traveling through Asia underscored that message, with a vengeance.

Superficially, Japan's boom of the 1980s seems like China's today. Yes, both happened in Asia, both led to mammoth trade imbalances, both arose from combined governmental and private-industrial efforts, and both unnerved the United States. But the differences are more numerous than the similarities, and more important. Japan was and is rich; for China, that is decades away. Japan's debut as an international host with its Olympic Games was already 20 years in the past (Tokyo, 1964); China's is still ahead. To me the most striking difference was cultural and moralistic: specifically, Japan's cocksureness. Japan and many neighboring nations saw its rise as a challenge to the American idea, and they didn't care who knew it. No one thinks that today's China lacks cultural confidence. By now I should have programmed auto-text keys to use when transcribing interviews, so that I can plug in the rote passage about "our 5,000 years of history" or "the world's longest continuous civilization" with one stroke. But I have encountered virtually no lecturing from Chinese friends, officials, students, passersby, or interviewees.

People inside China have a vivid sense of the whack-a-mole challenge they face at every level. For rural people, staying alive. For the urban employed class, finding enough money to pay for an apartment (with prices soaring), get kids into school (also expensive, with fees required even at public schools), fend off health emergencies (ditto), plus somehow save enough for retirement (in the midst of a huge demographic shift, driven by the one-child policy, toward a society with many more dependents and many fewer active workers). For company officials, managing China's current "brand image" disaster, plus the soaring costs of water, energy, and raw materials, plus the competition from thousands of other companies just like them. For regional officials, fending off complaints about pollution and corruption while still bringing in jobs. For the national government, managing all this and political and international crises too. Based on their record over the last 20 years, Chinese at all levels will probably find a way to stay just ahead of these disasters. But the situation doesn't leave many people I've met sounding boastful.

Japan was not like this. By the time I arrived there in 1986, Ezra Vogel's famed *Japan as Number One* had been on the market for several years. Vogel was arguing that many of Japan's practices deserved to be examined as influential new world models. But because of the title, the book was easily misunderstood as suggesting that Japan had actually become the No. 1 power. That was certainly the preferred interpretation of many of the Japanese officials and intellectuals I interviewed. For them, Japan and its concepts had won, which explicitly meant that America and its ideas had lost.

This attitude showed up even when I wasn't looking for it. In Tokyo in 1989, I was summoned to meet Shintaro Ishihara, a bluff Pat Buchanan–like politician who was later elected governor of Tokyo. He was famous then for his book (written with Akio Morita) *No to Ieru Nippon*, or *The Japan*

That Can Say No, which argued that Japan finally had the muscle to tell America to shut up. Behind it was the conceit that America had reached its crest—not just geostrategically, with its costly military commitments, nor just commercially, with the shoddy products it brought to market and its selfish refusal to save or conserve. Rather, America's failure involved its very essence, its fitness as a culture to compete. His book contrasted the chaos, disorder, and preening individualism that characterized America with the unity, harmony, and unspoken communication that supposedly made the Japanese into one smoothly functioning productive team. ("Supposedly" because, as Karel van Wolferen and other foreign critics noted, the "naturally" cooperative nature of Japanese society generally resulted from a firm system of incentives and constraints.) As applied to those inherent traits, "America in decline" was not an accusation but an assumed fact.

At one level, the Japanese claim of superior fitness raised worthy analytic issues. Twice in its history, Japan has achieved something not even modern China can claim: full technological parity with the mighty nations of the West. (The first was in the decades after Commodore Perry's arrival, when it modernized frantically to avoid the colonial humiliation that had befallen China; the second, of course, was after World War II.) But it was not Japan's strategy of "developmental economics" that constituted its real challenge to the American idea—American strategists from Alexander Hamilton to Vannevar Bush would have felt perfectly at home with the idea of using state power to stimulate the growth of private industrial technologies. The racial and political elements of the Japanese model were something else again.

What did this mean for the American idea, or my understanding of it? From its start, America had been a rowdy place, the consequence of continually making room for new people, plans, and ideas. There was no sense in trying to be a second-rate Japan, though specific details in its economic and social approach ("patient capital," improving K–12 education) deserved close study. America's hope was to be more fully American—not more like them, our competitors, but *More Like Us*, as I called one book I wrote from Japan. That in turn meant more support for innovation, more embrace of immigration, more acceptance of the churn of dynamic disorder, more of the kind of public help—the GI Bill, public schools—that gave as many people as possible a fair chance. The American idea, as I saw it from Japan, was strength through radically opened opportunity. The good parts of the boom of the 1990s, the parts that preceded the bubble, were consistent with this approach: more room for immigrant talent, more public support for Americans seeking a second and third chance, balanced budgets to reduce the overhang of debt. The natural effect of globalization is to make all of these more difficult, as some people get richer (through an ever-larger market for their financial, corporate, professional, or entertainment skills) and others with less specialized skills have to adapt more quickly to keep up. The inevitable rise of new barriers makes it all the more important to keep removing as many barriers as we can.

When I came to China, I naturally wondered if this might be the great challenger to the American idea. Certainly it has the scale to challenge almost anything it chooses. Barring catastrophe, sooner or later China will have the world's largest economy. That won't mean as much as it sounds: Since China has four times as many people as America, it need only reach one-fourth of America's per capita income to be No. 1 in total output. (The ratio now is something like one-seventh or one-sixth, depending on how you calculate and whose Chinese statistics you believe.) I've never heard a Chinese authority assert that China could draw even, in per capita terms, in the foreseeable future.

Is China warming up for the kind of challenge Americans fear? I know it can look that way. As I listen to U.S. discussion from afar, I hear the references to China's growing "soft power" (such reports are rarely filed by people based here), to its rising military budget (still a small fraction of America's), to the power it has gained through its hoard of U.S. dollars, to its confident assertions about the success of its upcoming Olympic Games, and to other signs of its potential chest-thumping. All I can report is how different the same issues seem here and how much less boastful talk I have encountered than I would have expected, and than I did in other parts of Asia during the previous Asian boom.

Yes, if you try hard enough, you can get some Chinese intellectuals or officials to say that their system might in some ways be proving itself "superior," as would befit a society with a 5,000-year heritage, etc. (Where is that auto-text key?) I've talked several times with a senior party official in Beijing who said that China's material success will eventually command respect for the political and cultural ideas that lie behind it. The first time I was summoned to see him, I was very nervous. I was told to come to Beijing for a meeting, and as I was whisked to the official's quarters in a shiny black Audi A8 (the car of the commissars) that blasted other traffic out of the way with a deafening Klaxon, I thought: This does not bode well. But the official, who turned out to be a friend of a Chinese friend of mine, wanted to talk about religion's role in public life: how it worked in America, how it might return to China. In many hours of subsequent talks, the very closest to a triumphal or scolding note I heard from him involved the practical problems of today's U.S.-style democracy.

"In the long run, China must be democratic," he told me on my latest visit. Everyone says that—without saying how many lifetimes away the "long run" might be. But even as China becomes democratic, this man said, it will need to be cautious about following every detail of a U.S. model. He talked about the Florida recount nightmare of the 2000 election and the crippling, constant need for American candidates to raise money. "I have observed that in Western democracy, those elected do not represent the general public," he said, Chomsky-like. And even when they do, "between elections you get maybe two years of stability to do any real work, then the campaigning begins again! The constant campaigns are a cost society has to pay." Even if you construed this as "anti-American"—as opposed to "accurate"—it is a far cry from what the likes of Shintaro Ishihara said when dancing on the corpse of the decadent U.S.

Yes, some Chinese intellectuals argue seriously that the country's rise proves the new vitality of Confucian truths. So, they suggest, this century, or the next one, or some future one ("It could take five hundred years," my party-boss friend says) could be the era of world recognition of the great Asian traditions: Confucianism, Taoism, and Buddhism. And for a final yes, if you try really hard, you can look for other rumblings suggesting China's great-power ambitions.

There is also the peculiar nature of today's "Chinese idea." I'll explore this topic more fully another time, but the most urgent axis of debate appears to be whether China stands for any "idea" at all. Many academics wring their hands about "kids today" who only want to get jobs with the most prestigious international companies and buy the fanciest cars; others say that's just a trend, that religion (or Confucianism, or Marxism, or something) will come back. Still others say that for the foreseeable future, it would be perverse for China to be distracted by any but practical concerns, since it has so much work to do there, especially on its environment.

What no one seems to contend is that China should be readying a major vision to impose on the world. Over the months, I've asked students, professors, public officials, and businesspeople versions of these questions: When China is strong, what will it want of the world? What will it expect of other countries? Practically by birthright, Americans can answer such a question about America's expectations of the world. We want liberty; we want democracy; we have, as

George W. Bush put it in his second inaugural address, the "great objective of ending tyranny." Whether by birthright or by current circumstances, few Chinese people have any answer to this question. Usually I am greeted with a puzzled or polite silence. If there is a response, it is something like "recognition." Or "respect."

I am not saying that a year's exposure to China has made me complacent or triumphalist. Through scale alone, China will be a handful. As I argued in the chapter about China's emergence as the world's factory ("China Makes, the World Takes"), Americans need to be actively thinking about how to protect their economic interests when dealing with China, how to help China limit its air and water pollution before it's too late for everyone, and how to engage China constructively in other ways.

But I am saying that for now, Americans shouldn't worry about an ideological challenge from China, or whether China's economic rise will soon mean the preeminence of the "Chinese idea." The people and leaders of China have too much else on their minds. What I've learned from China, so far, is that instead of girding to defend the American idea against some new foreign challenge, we should take the opportunity to shore it up, in three ways.

The first way is ensuring a particular kind of openness, which at all times has been the essence of America. The country needs to keep making room for its own people, while also continuing to make room for people from outside. It's not easy to achieve both goals, since in the short run, they conflict. The Americans most likely to be muscled aside by hungry outside talent are those with the odds against them in other ways. That's a reality. Rather than ignore the tension or use it as an excuse to close the borders, we have to find a way to reduce it. Otherwise, we cut off one of the two strengths (the other being military power) that no other country can possibly match.

A leading Chinese university, Jiao Tong of Shanghai, publishes an annual ranking of the best universities in the world, based on their research excellence. This is a soberer assessment than the fanciful "Best College" charts in U.S. magazines, and it emphasizes America's complete dominance of the field. On the latest Jiao Tong list, America has eight of the top 10 positions (exceptions: Cambridge and Oxford in England), and 17 of the top 20. (The other exception: the University of Tokyo, at 20.) China has zero of the top 100, and Japan has six. When I asked a Jiao Tong professor about the ranking, he said it was unfairly skewed, because American universities can take talent from everywhere else. *Yes*. We have to keep it that way, and for more than just universities.

Second is being idealistic but not consistent—or not foolishly consistent, as one of *The Atlantic Monthly's* founders put it 150 years ago. The United States can't and shouldn't be a status quo power. Consciously or not, most Americans believe that as the rest of the world modernizes, in crucial ways it will come to resemble us more and more. Let's skip for a moment the reasons why that belief is silly and instead recognize that it is very strong. It is part of our founding principle. The Declaration of Independence spoke of "the course of human events," not the complaints of the American colonists. The constant arrival of immigrants reminds us that people from around the world actually do want to become Americans. (A few hours before writing this, I heard from a young woman in the hinterland of Sichuan province: "My dream, to go to America!") Globalization has had a large Americanizing component—that's part of the complaint against it. While any sensible person wants to learn as much from other cultures as possible, Americans are bound to think that we have something to tell others about individual potential, about the idea of equality, about respect for civil liberties. The rest of the world understands this, which is why our recent infringements on our own civil liberties are so damaging to our image worldwide.

But retaining that idea doesn't mean believing two apparently consistent corollaries: that everyone else actually does want to be like us, and that it is within our power to force or entice them to. Believing this makes us believe that other countries—Japan a generation ago, China today—are just about to become America-like, and that if they resist, they can be forced to comply. (To say nothing of Iraq.) Speak for our values, yes, and clearly. Be deluded about them, no.

Finally, we should display the confidence, good humor, and thick-skinnedness befitting a country of our stature. When living in Japan, I heard accounts from many Japanese who had gone to the U.S. for business or study in the 1950s, after the Allied occupation ended. They looked at the factories and the farms and the vastness of America and asked themselves: What were we thinking? How could tiny Japan have imagined challenging the United States? After the Soviet Union fell and the hollowness of its system was exposed, many Americans asked: What were we thinking about "two superpower" competition with the U.S.S.R.? Its missiles were lethal and its ideology was brutal and dangerous. But a rival to America as an overall model? John F. Kennedy was only one of many to suggest as much, in his 1960 campaign references to the prestige gap as well as missile gap that had opened. Eventually, we all learned there had been no comparison at all. I think if more Americans came to China right now and saw how hard so many of its people are struggling just to survive, they too might ask: What are we thinking in considering China an overall threat? Yes, its factories are formidable, and its weight in the world is huge. But this is still a big, poor, developing nation trying to solve the emergency of the moment. Susan Shirk, of the University of California at San Diego, recently published a very insightful book that calls China a "fragile superpower." "When I discuss it in America," she told me, "people always ask, 'What do you mean, *fragile*?'" When she discusses it here in China, "they always ask, 'What do you mean, *superpower*?'"

Foreign examples are useful spurs to internal action. Sputnik served that purpose 50 years ago, and Japan's industrial successes led to valuable changes in American corporate and fiscal practices nearly a generation ago. A look at China can help America address its main shortcomings—reckless fiscal and foreign policies, delay in moving away from dependence on oil—and perhaps also suggest ways the nations can work together on challenges, mainly environmental, that threaten them and others.

But let's not panic. Let's show the patient confidence—Lincoln, Marshall, Eisenhower—that is part of the American idea. Let's not look for slights or imagined insults to react to. Among our worst enemies at the moment is our own hair-trigger mentality about foreign challenge, and the enemies that outlook generates. Our idea is strong. We should act as if we know that.

THE $1.4 TRILLION QUESTION

JANUARY 2008

Stephen Schwarzman may think he has image problems in America. He is the cofounder and CEO of the Blackstone Group, and he threw himself a $3 million party for his sixtieth birthday in 2007, shortly before making many hundreds of millions of dollars in his company's IPO and finding clever ways to avoid paying taxes. That's nothing compared with the way he looks in China. Here, he and his company are surprisingly well-known, thanks to blogs, newspapers, and talk-show references. In America, Schwarzman's perceived offense is greed—a sin we readily forgive and forget. In China, the suspicion is that he has somehow hoodwinked ordinary Chinese people out of their hard-earned cash.

Last June, China's Blackstone investment was hailed in the American press as a sign of canny sophistication. It seemed just the kind of thing the U.S. government had in mind when it hammered China to use its new wealth as a "responsible stakeholder" among nations. By putting $3 billion of China's national savings into the initial public offering of America's best-known private-equity firm, the Chinese government allied itself with a big-time Western firm without raising political fears by trying to buy operating control (it bought only 8 percent of Blackstone's shares, and nonvoting shares at that). The contrast with the Japanese and Saudis, who in their nouveau riche phase roused irritation and envy with their showy purchases of Western brand names and landmark properties, was plain.

Six months later, it didn't look so canny, at least not financially. China's Blackstone holdings lost, on paper, about $1 billion, during a time when the composite index of the Shanghai Stock Exchange was soaring. At two different universities where I've spoken recently, students have pointed out that Schwarzman was a major Republican donor. A student at Fudan University knew a detail I didn't: that in 2007 President Bush attended a Republican National Committee fund-raiser at Schwarzman's apartment in Manhattan (think what he would have made of the fact that Schwarzman, who was one year behind Bush at Yale, had been a fellow member of Skull and Bones). Wasn't the whole scheme a way to take money from the Chinese people and give it to the president's crony?

The Blackstone case is titillating in its personal detail, but it is also an unusually clear and personalized symptom of a deeper, less publicized, and potentially much more destructive tension in U.S.–China relations. It's not just Stephen Schwarzman's company that the *laobaixing*, the ordinary Chinese masses, have been subsidizing. It's everyone in the United States.

Through the quarter century in which China has been opening to world trade, Chinese leaders have deliberately held down living standards for their own people and propped them up in the United States. This is the real meaning of the vast trade surplus—$1.4 trillion and counting, going up by about $1 billion per day—that the Chinese government has mostly parked in U.S. Treasury notes. In effect, every person in the (rich) United States has over the past 10 years or so borrowed about $4,000 from someone in the (poor) People's Republic of China. Like so many imbalances in economics, this one can't go on indefinitely, and therefore won't. But the way it ends—suddenly versus gradually, for predictable reasons versus during a panic—will make an enormous difference to the U.S. and Chinese economies over the next few years, to say nothing of bystanders in Europe and elsewhere.

Any economist will say that Americans have been living better than they should—which is by definition the case when a nation's total consumption is greater than its total production, as America's now is. Economists will also point out that, despite the glitter of China's big cities and the rise of its billionaire class, China's people have been living far worse than they could. That's what it means when a nation consumes only half of what it produces, as China does. Neither government likes to draw attention to this arrangement, because it has been so convenient on both sides. For China, it has helped the regime guide development in the way it would like—and keep the domestic economy's growth rate from crossing the thin line that separates "unbelievably fast" from "uncontrollably inflationary." For America, it has meant cheaper iPods, lower interest rates, reduced mortgage payments, a lighter tax burden. But because of political tensions in both countries, and because of the huge and growing size of the imbalance, the arrangement now shows signs of cracking apart.

In the article "Countdown to a Meltdown," published in the July/August 2005 issue of *The Atlantic*, I described an imagined future in which a real-estate crash and shakiness in the U.S. credit markets led to panic by Chinese and other foreign investors, with unpleasant effects for years to come. The real world has recently had inklings of similar concerns. In late 2007, relative nobodies in China's establishment were able to cause brief panics in the foreign-exchange markets merely by hinting that China might stop supplying so much money to the United States. In August 2007, an economic researcher named He Fan, who works at the Chinese Academy of Social Sciences and did part of his doctoral research at Harvard, suggested in an op-ed piece in *China Daily* that if the U.S. dollar kept collapsing in value, China might move some of its holdings into stronger currencies. This was presented not as a threat but as a statement of the obvious, like saying that during a market panic, lots of people sell. The column quickly provoked alarmist stories in Europe and America suggesting that China was considering the "nuclear option"—unloading its dollars.

A few months later, a veteran politician named Cheng Siwei suggested essentially the same thing He Fan had. Cheng, in his mid-seventies, was trained as a chemical engineer and has no official role in setting Chinese economic policy. But within hours of his speech, a flurry of trading forced the dollar to what was then its lowest level against the euro and other currencies. The headline in the *South China Morning Post* the next day was: "Officials' Words Shrivel U.S. Dollar." Expressing amazement at the markets' response, Carl Weinberg, chief economist at the High Frequency Economics advisory group, said, "This would be kind of like Congressman Charlie Rangel giving a speech telling the Fed to hike or cut interest rates." (Cheng, like Rangel, is known for colorful comments—but he is less powerful, since Rangel after all chairs the House Committee on Ways and Means.) In the following weeks, phrases like "run on the dollar" and "collapse of confidence" showed up more and more frequently in financial newsletters. The nervousness only increased when someone who does have influence, Chinese Premier Wen Jiabao, said in November 2007, "We are worried about how to preserve the value" of China's dollar holdings.

When the dollar is strong, the following (good) things happen: the price of food, fuel, imports, manufactured goods, and just about everything else (vacations in Europe!) goes down. The value of the stock market, real estate, and just about all other American assets goes up. Interest rates go down—for mortgage loans, credit-card debt, and commercial borrowing. Tax rates can be lower, since foreign lenders hold down the cost of financing the national debt. The only problem is that American-made goods become more expensive for foreigners, so the country's exports are hurt.

When the dollar is weak, the following (bad) things happen: the price of food, fuel, imports, and so on (no more vacations in Europe) goes up. The value of the stock market, real estate, and just about all other American assets goes down. Interest rates are higher. Tax rates can be higher, to cover the increased cost of financing the national debt. The only benefit is that American-made goods become cheaper for foreigners, which helps create new jobs and can raise the value of export-oriented American firms (winemakers in California, producers of medical devices in New England).

The dollar's value has been high for many years—unnaturally high, in large part because of the implicit bargain with the Chinese. Living standards in China, while rising rapidly, have by the same logic been unnaturally low. To understand why this situation probably can't go on, and what might replace it—via a dollar crash or some other event—let's consider how this curious balance of power arose and how it works.

WHY A POOR COUNTRY HAS SO MUCH MONEY

By 1996, China amassed its first $100 billion in foreign assets, mainly held in U.S. dollars. (China considers these holdings a state secret, so all numbers come from analyses by outside experts.) By 2001, that sum doubled to about $200 billion, according to Edwin Truman of the Peterson Institute for International Economics in Washington. Since then, it has increased more than sixfold, to well over a trillion dollars, and China's foreign reserves are now the largest in the world. (In second place is Japan, whose economy is, at official exchange rates, nearly twice as large as China's but which has only two-thirds the foreign assets; the next-largest after that are the United Arab Emirates and Russia.) China's U.S. dollar assets probably account for about 70 percent of its foreign holdings, according to the latest analyses by Brad Setser, a former Treasury Department economist now with the Council on Foreign Relations; the rest are mainly in euros, plus some yen. Most of China's U.S. investments are in conservative, low-yield instruments like Treasury notes and federal-agency bonds, rather than showier Blackstone-style bets. Because notes and bonds backed by the U.S. government are considered the safest investments in the world, they pay lower interest than corporate bonds, and for the past two years their annual interest payments of 4 to 5 percent have barely matched the 5 to 6 percent decline in the U.S. dollar's value versus the RMB.

Americans sometimes debate (though not often) whether in principle it is good to rely so heavily on money controlled by a foreign government. The debate has never been more relevant, because America has never before been so deeply in debt to one country. Meanwhile, the Chinese are having a debate of their own—about whether the deal makes sense for them. Certainly China's officials are aware that their stock purchases prop up 401(k) values, their money-market holdings keep down American interest rates, and their bond purchases do the same thing—plus allow our government to spend money without raising taxes.

"From a distance, this, to say the least, is strange," Lawrence Summers, the former Secretary of the Treasury and president of Harvard, told me in 2007 in Shanghai. He was referring to the oddity that a country with so many of its own needs still unmet would let "this $1 trillion go to a mature, old, rich place from a young, dynamic place."

It's more than strange. Some Chinese people are rich, but China as a whole is unbelievably short on many of the things that qualify countries as fully developed. Shanghai has about the same climate as Washington, D.C.—and its public schools have no heating. (Go to a classroom when it's cold, and you'll see 40 children, all in their winter jackets, their breath forming clouds in the air.) Beijing is more like Boston. On winter nights, thousands of people mass along the curbsides of major thoroughfares, enduring long waits and fighting their way onto hopelessly overcrowded public buses that then spend hours stuck on jammed roads. And these are the showcase cities! In rural Gansu province, I have seen schools where 18 junior high school girls share a single dormitory room, sleeping shoulder to shoulder, sardine-style.

Better schools, more abundant parks, better health care, cleaner air and water, better sewers in the cities—you name it, and if it isn't in some way connected to the factory-export economy, China hasn't got it, or not enough. This is true at the personal level, too. The average cash income for workers in a big factory is about $160 per month. On the farm, it's a small fraction of that. Most people in China feel they are moving up, but from a very low starting point.

So why is China shipping its money to America? An economist would describe the oddity by saying that China has by far the highest national savings in the world. This sounds admirable, but when taken to an extreme—as in China—it indicates an economy out of sync with the rest of the world, and one that is deliberately keeping its own people's living standards lower than they could be. For comparison, India's savings rate is about 25 percent, which in effect means that India's people consume 75 percent of what they collectively produce. (Reminder from Econ 101: The savings rate is the net share of national output either exported or saved and invested for consumption in the future. Effectively, it's what your own people produce but don't use.) For Korea and Japan, the savings rate is typically from the high 20s to the mid-30s. Recently, America's has at times been below zero, which means that it consumes, via imports, more than it makes.

China's savings rate is a staggering 50 percent, which is probably unprecedented in any country during peacetime. This doesn't mean that the average family is saving half of its earnings—though the personal savings rate in China is also very high. Much of China's national income is "saved" almost invisibly and kept in the form of foreign assets. Until now, most Chinese have willingly put up with this, because the economy has been growing so fast that even a suppressed level of consumption improves most people's quality of life year by year.

But saying that China has a high savings rate describes the situation without explaining it. Why should the Communist Party of China countenance a policy that takes so much wealth from the world's poor, in their own country, and gives it to the United States? To add to the mystery, why should China be content to put so many of its holdings into dollars, knowing that the dollar is virtually guaranteed to keep losing value against the RMB? And how long can its people tolerate being denied so much of their earnings, when they and their country need so much? The Chinese government did not explicitly set out to tighten the belt on its population while offering cheap money to American home owners. But the fact that it does results directly from explicit choices it *has* made—two in particular. Both arise from crucial controls the government maintains over an economy that in many other ways has become wide open. The situation may be easiest to explain by following a U.S. dollar on its journey from a customer's hand in America to a factory in China and back again to the T-note auction in the United States.

THE VOYAGE OF A DOLLAR

Let's say you buy an Oral-B electric toothbrush for $30 at a CVS in the United States. I choose this example because I've seen a factory in China that probably made the toothbrush. Most of that $30 stays in America, with CVS, the distributors, and Oral-B itself. Eventually $3 or so—an average percentage for small consumer goods—makes its way back to southern China.

When the factory originally placed its bid for Oral-B's business, it stated the price in dollars: X million toothbrushes for Y dollars each. But the Chinese manufacturer can't use the dollars directly. It needs RMB—to pay the workers their 1,200-RMB [about $175 in 2008] monthly salary, to buy supplies from other factories in China, to pay its taxes. So it takes the dollars to the local commercial bank—let's say the Shenzhen Development Bank. After showing receipts or way-bills to prove that it earned the dollars in genuine trade, not as speculative inflow, the factory trades them for RMB.

This is where the first controls kick in. In other major countries, the counterparts to the Shenzhen Development Bank can decide for themselves what to do with the dollars they take in. Trade them for euros or yen on the foreign-exchange market? Invest them directly in America? Issue dollar loans? Whatever they think will bring the highest return. But under China's "surrender requirements," Chinese banks can't do those things. They must treat the dollars, in effect, as contraband, and turn most or all of them (instructions vary from time to time) over to China's equivalent of the Federal Reserve bank, the People's Bank of China, for RMB at whatever is the official rate of exchange.

With thousands of transactions per day, the dollars pile up like crazy at the PBOC—more precisely, by more than a billion dollars per day. They pile up even faster than the trade surplus with America would indicate, because customers in many other countries settle their accounts in dollars, too.

The PBOC must do something with that money, and current Chinese doctrine allows it only one option: to give the dollars to another arm of the central government, the State Administration of Foreign Exchange. It is then SAFE's job to figure out where to park the dollars for the best return: so much in U.S. stocks, so much shifted to euros, and the great majority left in the boring safety of U.S. Treasury notes.

And thus our dollar comes back home. Spent at CVS, passed

to Oral-B, paid to the factory in southern China, traded for RMB at the Shenzhen bank, "surrendered" to the PBOC, passed to SAFE for investment, and then bid at auction for Treasury notes, it is ready to be reinjected into the U.S. money supply and spent again—ideally on Chinese-made goods.

At no point did an ordinary Chinese person decide to send so much money to America. In fact, at no point was most of this money at his or her disposal at all. These are in effect enforced savings, which are the result of the two huge and fundamental choices made by the central government.

One is to dictate the RMB's value relative to other currencies, rather than allow it to be set by forces of supply and demand, as are the values of the dollar, euro, pound, etc. The obvious reason for doing this is to keep Chinese-made products cheap, so Chinese factories will stay busy. This is what Americans have in mind when they complain that the Chinese government is rigging the world currency markets. And there are numerous less obvious reasons. The very act of managing a currency's value may be a more important distorting factor than the exact rate at which it is set. As for the rate—the subject of much U.S. lecturing—given the huge difference in living standards between China and the United States, even a big rise in the RMB's value would leave China with a price advantage over manufacturers elsewhere. (If the RMB doubled against the dollar, a factory worker might go from earning $160 per month to $320—not enough to send many jobs back to America, though enough to hurt China's export economy.) Once a government decides to thwart the market-driven exchange rate of its currency, it must control countless other aspects of its financial system, through instruments like surrender requirements and the equally ominous-sounding "sterilization bonds" (a way of keeping foreign-currency swaps from creating inflation, as they otherwise could).

These and similar tools are the way China's government imposes an unbelievably high savings rate on its people. The result, while very complicated, is to keep the buying power earned through China's exports out of the hands of Chinese consumers as a whole. Individual Chinese people certainly have gotten their hands on a lot of buying power, notably the billionaire entrepreneurs who have attracted the world's attention (see "Mr. Zhang Builds His Dream Town"). But when it comes to amassing international reserves, what matters is that China as a whole spends so little of what it earns, even as some Chinese people spend a lot.

The other major decision is not to use more money to address China's needs directly—by building schools and agricultural research labs, cleaning up toxic waste, what have you. Both decisions stem from the central government's vision of what is necessary to keep China on its unprecedented path of growth. The government doesn't want to let the market set the value of the RMB, because it thinks that would disrupt the constant growth and the course it has carefully and expensively set for the factory-export economy. In the short run, it worries that the RMB's value against the dollar and the euro would soar, pricing some factories in "expensive" places such as Shanghai out of business. In the long run, it views an unstable currency as a nuisance in itself, since currency fluctuation makes everything about business with the outside world more complicated. Companies have a harder time predicting overseas revenues, negotiating contracts, luring foreign investors, or predicting the costs of fuel, component parts, and other imported goods.

And the government doesn't want to increase domestic spending dramatically, because it fears that improving average living conditions could paradoxically intensify the rich-poor tensions that are China's major social problem. The country is already covered with bulldozers, wrecking balls, and construction cranes, all to keep the manufacturing machine steaming ahead. Trying to build anything more at the moment—sewage-treatment plants, for a start, which would mean a better life for its own people, or smokestack scrubbers and related "clean" technology, which would start to address the world pollution for which China is increasingly held responsible—would likely just drive prices up, intensifying inflation and thus reducing the already minimal purchasing power of most workers. Food prices have been rising so fast that they have led to riots. In November 2007, a large Carrefour grocery in Chongqing offered a limited-time sale of vegetable oil, at 20 percent (11 RMB, or about $1.50) off the normal price per bottle. Three people were killed and 31 injured in a stampede toward the shelves.

This is the bargain China has made—rather, the one its leaders have imposed on its people. They'll keep creating new factory jobs, and thus reduce China's own social tensions and create opportunities for its rural poor. The Chinese will live better year by year, though not as well as they could. And they'll be protected from the risk of potentially catastrophic hyperinflation, which might undo what the nation's decades of growth have built. In exchange, the government will hold much of the nation's wealth in paper assets in the United States, thereby preventing a run on the dollar, shoring up relations between China and America, and sluicing enough cash back into Americans' hands to let the spending go on.

WHAT THE CHINESE HOPE WILL HAPPEN

The Chinese public is beginning to be aware that its government is sitting on a lot of money—money not being spent to help China directly, money not doing so well in Blackstone-style foreign investments, money invested in the ever-falling U.S. dollar. Chinese bloggers and press commentators have begun making a connection between the billions of dollars the country is sending away and the domestic needs the country has not addressed. There is more and more pressure to show that the return on foreign investments is worth China's sacrifice—and more and more potential backlash against bets that don't pay off. (While the Chinese government need not stand for popular election, it generally tries to reduce sources of popular discontent when it can.) The public is beginning to behave like the demanding client of an investment adviser: It wants better returns, with fewer risks.

This is the challenge facing Lou Jiwei and Gao Xiqing, who will play a larger role in the U.S. economy than Americans are accustomed to from foreigners. Lou, a longtime Communist Party official in his late fifties, is the chairman of the new

China Investment Corporation, which is supposed to find creative ways to increase returns on at least $200 billion of China's foreign assets. He is influential within the party but has little international experience. Thus the financial world's attention has turned to Gao Xiqing, who is the CIC's general manager.

Twenty years ago, after graduating from Duke Law School, Gao was the first Chinese citizen to pass the New York state bar exam. He returned to China in 1988, after several years as an associate at the New York law firm Mudge Rose (Richard Nixon's old firm), to teach securities law and help develop China's newly established stock markets. By local standards, he is hip. At an economics conference in Beijing in December 2007, other Chinese speakers wore boxy dark suits. Gao, looking fit in his mid-fifties, wore a tweed jacket and black turtleneck, an Ironman-style multifunction sports watch on his wrist.

Under Lou and Gao, the CIC started with a bang with Blackstone—the wrong kind of bang. Now, many people suggest, it may be chastened enough to take a more careful approach. Indeed, that was the message it sent in late 2007, with news that its next round of investments would be in China's own banks, to shore up some with credit problems. And it looks to be studying aggressive but careful ways to manage huge sums. About the time the CIC was making the Blackstone deal, its leadership and staff undertook a crash course in modern financial markets. They hired the international consulting firm McKinsey to prepare confidential reports about the way they should organize themselves and the investment principles they should apply. They hired Booz Allen Hamilton to prepare similar reports, so they could compare the two. Yet another consulting firm, Towers Perrin, provided advice, especially about staffing and pay. The CIC leaders commissioned studies of other large state-run investment funds—in Norway, Singapore, the Gulf States, Alaska—to see which approaches worked and which didn't. They were fascinated by the way America's richest universities managed their endowments and ordered multiple copies of *Pioneering Portfolio Management*, by David Swensen, who as Yale's chief investment officer has guided its endowment to sustained and rapid growth. Last summer, teams from the CIC made long study visits to Yale and Duke universities, among others.

Gao Xiqing and other CIC officials have avoided discussing their plans publicly. "If you tell people ahead of time what you're going to do—well, you just can't operate that way in a market system," he said at his Beijing appearance. "What I can say is, we'll play by the international rules, and we'll be responsible investors." Gao emphasized several times how much the CIC had to learn: "We're the new kids on the block. Because of media attention, there is huge pressure on us—we're already under water now." The words "under water" were in natural-sounding English, and clearly referred to Blackstone.

Others familiar with the CIC say that its officials are coming to appreciate the unusual problems they will face. For instance, any investment group needs to be responsible to outside supervisors, and the trick for the CIC will be to make itself accountable to Communist Party leadership without becoming a mere conduit for favored investment choices by party bosses. How can it attract the best talent? Does it want to staff up quickly, to match its quickly mounting assets, by bidding for financial managers on the world market—where many of the candidates are high-priced, not fluent in Chinese, and reluctant to move to Beijing? Or can it afford to take the time to home-grow its own staff?

While the CIC is figuring out its own future, outsiders are trying to figure out the CIC—and also SAFE, which will continue handling many of China's assets. As far as anyone can tell, the starting point for both is risk avoidance. No more Blackstones. No more CNOOC-Unocals. (In 2005, the Chinese state oil firm CNOOC attempted to buy U.S.-based Unocal. It withdrew the offer in the face of intense political opposition to the deal in America.) One person involved with the CIC said that its officials had seen recent Lou Dobbs broadcasts criticizing "Communist China" and were "shell-shocked" about the political resentment their investments might encounter in the United States. For all these reasons the Chinese leadership, as another person put it, "has a strong preference to follow someone else's lead, not in an imitative way," but as an unobtrusive minority partner wherever possible. It will follow the lead of others for now, that is, while the CIC takes its first steps as a gigantic international financial investor.

The latest analyses by Brad Setser suggest that despite all the talk about abandoning the dollar, China is still putting about as large a share of its money into dollars as ever, somewhere between 65 and 70 percent of its foreign earnings. "Politically, the last thing they want is to signal a loss of faith in the dollar," Andy Rothman, of the financial firm CLSA, told me. That would lead to a surge in the RMB, which would hurt Chinese exporters, not to mention the damage it would cause to China's vast existing dollar assets.

The problem is that these and other foreign observers must guess at China's aims, rather than knowing for sure. As Rothman put it, "The opaqueness about intentions and goals is always the issue." The mini-panics last year took hold precisely because no one could be sure that SAFE was not about to change course.

The uncertainty arises in part from the limited track record of China's new financial leadership. As one American financier pointed out to me, "The man in charge of the whole thing"—Lou Jiwei—"has never bought a share of stock, never bought a car, never bought a house." Another foreign financier said, after meeting some CIC staffers, "By Chinese terms, these are very sophisticated people." But, he went on to say, in a professional sense none of them have lived through the financial crises of the last generation: the U.S. market crash of 1987, the "Asian flu" of the late 1990s, the collapse of the Internet bubble soon afterward. The Chinese economy was affected by all these upheavals, but the likes of Gao Xiqing were not fully exposed to their lessons, sheltered as they were within Chinese institutions.

Foreign observers also suggest that, even after exposure to the Lou Dobbs clips, the Chinese financial leadership may not yet fully grasp how suspicious other countries are likely to be of China's financial intentions, for reasons both fair and unfair. The unfair reason is all-purpose nervousness about any new rising power. "They need to understand, and they don't, that everything they do will be seen as political," a financier with extensive experience in both China and America told me. "Whatever they buy, whatever they say, whatever they do will be seen as China Inc."

The fair reason for concern is, again, the transparency problem. Twice in 2007, China in nonfinancial ways demonstrated the ripples that a nontransparent policy creates. In January, its military intentionally shot down one of its own satellites, filling orbital paths with debris. The exercise greatly alarmed the U.S. military, because of what seemed to be an implied threat to America's crucial space sensors. For several days, the Chinese government said nothing at all about the test, and nearly a year later, foreign analysts continued to debate whether it was a deliberate provocation, the result of a misunderstanding, or a freelance effort by the military. In November, China denied a U.S. navy aircraft carrier, the *Kitty Hawk*, routine permission to dock in Hong Kong for Thanksgiving, even though many navy families had gone there for a reunion. In each case, the most ominous aspect was that outsiders could not really be sure what the Chinese leadership had in mind. Were these deliberate taunts or shows of strength? The results of factional feuding within the leadership? Simple miscalculations? In the absence of clear official explanations, no one really knew, and many assumed the worst.

So it could be with finance, unless China becomes as transparent as it is rich. Chinese officials say they will move in that direction, but they're in no hurry. In fall 2007, Edwin Truman prepared a good-governance scorecard for dozens of "sovereign wealth" funds—government-run investment funds like SAFE and the CIC. He compared funds from Singapore, Korea, Norway, and elsewhere, ranking them on governing structure, openness, and similar qualities. China's funds ended up in the lower third of his list—better run than Iran's, Sudan's, or Algeria's, but worse than Mexico's, Russia's, or Kuwait's. China received no points in the "governance" category and half a point out of a possible 12 for "transparency and accountability."

Foreigners (and ordinary Chinese, too, for that matter) can't be sure about the mixture of political and strictly economic motives behind future investment decisions the Chinese leadership might make. When China's president, Hu Jintao, visited Seattle in 2006, he announced a large purchase of Boeing aircraft. When France's new president, Nicolas Sarkozy, visited China in late 2007, Hu announced an even larger purchase of Airbuses. Every Chinese order for an airplane is a political as well as commercial decision. Brad Setser says that the Chinese government probably believed that it would get "credit" for the Blackstone purchase in whatever negotiations came up next with the United States, in the same way it would get credit for choosing Boeing. This is another twist to the Kremlinology of trying to discern China's investment strategy.

Where the money goes, other kinds of power follow. Just ask Mikhail Gorbachev, as he reflects on the role bankruptcy played in bringing down the Soviet empire. While Japan's great wealth has not yet made it a major diplomatic actor, and China has so far shied from, rather than seized, opportunities to influence events outside its immediate realm, time and money could change that. China's military is too weak to challenge the U.S. directly, even in the Taiwan Strait, let alone anyplace else. That, too, could change.

A BALANCE OF TERROR

Let's take these fears about a rich, strong China to their logical extreme. The U.S. and Chinese governments are always disagreeing—about trade, foreign policy, the environment. Someday the disagreement could be severe. Taiwan, Tibet, North Korea, Iran—the possibilities are many, though Taiwan always heads the list. Perhaps a crackdown within China. Perhaps another accident, like the U.S. bombing of China's embassy in Belgrade in 1999, which everyone in China still believes was intentional and which no prudent American ever mentions here.

Whatever the provocation, China could consider its levers and weapons and find one stronger than all the rest—one no other country in the world can wield. Without China's billion dollars a day, the United States could not keep its economy stable or spare the dollar from collapse.

Would the Chinese use that weapon? The reasonable answer is no, because they would wound themselves grievously, too. Their years of national savings are held in the same dollars that would be ruined; in a panic, they'd get only a small share out before the value fell. Besides, their factories depend on customers with dollars to spend.

But that "reassuring" answer is actually frightening. Lawrence Summers calls today's arrangement "the balance of financial terror," and says that it is flawed in the same way that the "mutually assured destruction" of the Cold War era was. That doctrine held that neither the United States nor the Soviet Union would dare use its nuclear weapons against the other, since it would be destroyed in return. With allowances for hyperbole, something similar applies to the dollar stand-off. China can't afford to stop feeding dollars to America, because China's own dollar holdings would be devastated if it did. As long as that logic holds, the system works. As soon as it doesn't, we have a big problem.

What might poke a giant hole in that logic? Not necessarily a titanic struggle over the future of Taiwan. A simple mistake, for one thing. Another speech by Cheng Siwei—perhaps in response to a provocation by Lou Dobbs. A rumor that the oil economies are moving out of dollars for good, setting their prices in euros. Leaked suggestions that the Chinese government is hoping to buy Intel, leading to angry denunciations on the Capitol floor, leading to news that the Chinese will sit out the next Treasury auction. As many world tragedies have been caused by miscalculation as by malice.

Or pent-up political tensions, on all sides. China's lopsided growth—ahead in exports, behind in schooling, the environment, and everything else—makes the country socially less stable as it grows richer. Meanwhile, its expansion disrupts industries and provokes tensions in the rest of the world. The billions of dollars China pumps into the United States each week strangely seem to make it harder rather than easier for Americans to face their own structural problems. One day, something snaps. Suppose the CIC makes another bad bet—not another Blackstone but another WorldCom, with billions of dollars of Chinese people's assets irretrievably wiped out. They will need someone to blame, and Americans, for their part, are already primed to blame China back.

So, the shock comes. Does it inevitably cause a cataclysm? No one can know until it's too late. The important question to ask about the U.S.–China relationship, the economist Eswar Prasad, of Cornell, recently wrote in a paper about financial imbalances, is whether it has "enough flexibility to withstand and recover from large shocks, either internal or external." He suggested that the contained tensions are so great that the answer could be no.

Today's American system values upheaval; it's been a while since we've seen too much of it. But Americans who lived through the Depression knew the pain real disruption can bring. Today's Chinese, looking back on their country's last century, know, too. With a lack of tragic imagination, Americans have drifted into an arrangement that is comfortable while it lasts and could last for a while more. But not much longer.

Years ago, the Chinese might have averted today's pressures by choosing a slower and more balanced approach to growth. If they had it to do over again, I suspect they would in fact choose just the same path—they have gained so much, including the assets they can use to do what they have left undone, whenever the government chooses to spend them.

The same is not true, I suspect, for the United States, which might have chosen a very different path: less reliance on China's subsidies, more reliance on paying as we go. But it's a little late for those thoughts now. What's left is to prepare for what we find at the end of the path we have taken.

"THE CONNECTION HAS BEEN RESET"

MARCH 2008

Many foreigners who come to China for the Olympics will use the Internet to tell people back home what they have seen and to check what else has happened in the world.

The first thing they'll probably notice is that China's Internet seems slow. Partly this is because of congestion in China's internal networks, which affects domestic and international transmissions alike. Partly it is because even photons take a detectable period of time to travel beneath the Pacific Ocean to servers in America and back again; the trip to and from Europe is even longer, because that goes through America, too. And partly it is because of the delaying cycles imposed by China's system that monitors what people are looking for on the Internet, especially when they're looking overseas. That's what foreigners have heard about.

They'll likely be surprised, then, to notice that China's Internet seems surprisingly free and uncontrolled. Can they search for information about "Tibet independence" or "Tiananmen shooting" or other terms they have heard are taboo? Probably—and they'll be able to click right through to the controversial sites.

Even if they enter the Chinese-language term for "democracy in China," they'll probably get results. What about Wikipedia, famously off-limits to users in China? They will probably be able to reach it. Naturally the visitors will wonder: What's all this I've heard about the "Great Firewall" and China's tight limits on the Internet?

In reality, what the Olympic-era visitors will be discovering is not the absence of China's electronic control but its new refinement—a special Potemkin-style unfettered access that will be set up just for them, and just for the length of their stay. According to engineers I have spoken with at two tech organizations in China, the government bodies in charge of censoring the Internet have told them to get ready to unblock access from a list of specific Internet Protocol (IP) addresses—certain Internet cafés, access jacks in hotel rooms and conference centers where foreigners are expected to work or stay during the Olympic Games. (I am not giving names or identifying details of any Chinese citizens with whom I have discussed this topic, because they risk financial or criminal punishment for criticizing the system or even disclosing how it works. Also, I have not gone to Chinese government agencies for their side of the story, because the very existence of Internet controls is almost never discussed in public here, apart from vague statements about the importance of keeping online information "wholesome.")

Depending on how you look at it, the Chinese government's attempt to rein in the Internet is crude and slapdash or ingenious and well crafted. When American technologists write about the control system, they tend to emphasize its limits. When Chinese citizens discuss it—at least with me—they tend to emphasize its strength. All of them are right, which makes the government's approach to the Internet a nice proxy for its larger attempt to control people's daily lives.

Disappointingly, "Great Firewall" is not really the right term for the Chinese government's overall control strategy. China has indeed erected a firewall—a barrier to keep its Internet users from dealing easily with the outside world—but that is only one part of a larger, complex structure of monitoring and censorship. The official name for the entire approach, which is ostensibly a way to keep hackers and other rogue elements from harming Chinese Internet users, is the "Golden Shield Project." Since that term is too creepy to bear repeating, I'll use "the control system" for the overall strategy, which includes the "Great Firewall of China," or GFW, as the means of screening contact with other countries.

In America, the Internet was originally designed to be free of choke points, so that each packet of information could be routed quickly around any temporary obstruction. In China, the Internet came with choke points built in. Even now, virtually all Internet contact between China and the rest of the world is routed through a very small number of fiber-optic cables that enter the country at one of three points: the Beijing-Qingdao-Tianjin area in the north, where cables come in from Japan; Shanghai on the central coast, where they also come from Japan; and Guangzhou in the south, where they come from Hong Kong. (A few places in China have Internet service via satellite, but that is both expensive and slow.

Other lines run across Central Asia to Russia but carry little traffic.) In late 2006, Internet users in China were reminded just how important these choke points are when a seabed earthquake near Taiwan cut some major cables serving the country. It took months before international transmissions to and from most of China regained even their prequake speed, such as it was.

Thus Chinese authorities can easily do something that would be harder in most developed countries: physically monitor all traffic into or out of the country. They do so by installing at each of these few international gateways a device called a "tapper" or "network sniffer," which can mirror every packet of data going in or out. This involves mirroring in both a figurative and a literal sense. "Mirroring" is the term for normal copying or backup operations, and in this case real though extremely small mirrors are employed. Information travels along fiber-optic cables as little pulses of light, and as these travel through the Chinese gateway routers, numerous tiny mirrors bounce reflections of them to a separate set of "Golden Shield" computers. Here the term's creepiness is appropriate. As the other routers and servers (short for file servers, which are essentially very large-capacity computers) that make up the Internet do their best to get the packet where it's supposed to go, China's own surveillance computers are looking over the same information to see whether it should be stopped.

The mirroring routers were first designed and supplied to the Chinese authorities by the U.S. tech firm Cisco, which is why Cisco took such heat from human-rights organizations.

Cisco has always denied that it tailored its equipment to the authorities' surveillance needs, and said it merely sold them what it would sell anyone else. The issue is now moot, since similar routers are made by companies around the world, notably including China's own electronics giant, Huawei. The ongoing refinements are mainly in surveillance software, which the Chinese are developing themselves. Many of the surveillance engineers are thought to come from the military's own technology institutions. Their work is good and getting better, I was told by Chinese and foreign engineers who do "oppo research" on the evolving GFW to design better ways to get around it.

Andrew Lih, a former journalism professor and software engineer now based in Beijing (and author of the forthcoming book *The Wikipedia Story*), laid out for me the ways in which the GFW can keep an Internet user in China from finding desired material on a foreign site. In the few seconds after a user enters a request at the browser, and before something new shows up on the screen, at least four things can go wrong—or be made to go wrong.

The first and bluntest is the "DNS block." The DNS, or Domain Name System, is in effect the directory of Internet sites. Each time you enter a Web address, or URL—www.yahoo.com, let's say—the DNS looks up the IP address where the site can be found. IP addresses are numbers separated by dots—for example, theatlantic.com's is 38.118. 42.200. If the DNS is instructed to give back no address, or a bad address, the user can't reach the site in question—as a phone user could not make a call if given a bad number.

Typing in the URL for the BBC's main news site often gets the no-address treatment: If you try news.bbc.co.uk, you may get a "Site not found" message on the screen. For two months in 2002, Google's main site, google.com, got a different kind of bad-address treatment, which shunted users to its main competitor, the dominant Chinese search engine, Baidu. Chinese academics complained that this was hampering their work. The government, which does not have to stand for reelection but still tries not to antagonize important groups needlessly, let google.cn back online. During politically sensitive times, like the Seventeenth Communist Party Congress, many foreign sites have been temporarily shut down this way.

Next is the perilous "connect" phase. If the DNS has looked up and provided the right IP address, your computer sends a signal requesting a connection with that remote site. While your signal is going out, and as the other system is sending a reply, the surveillance computers within China are looking over your request, which has been mirrored to them. They quickly check a list of forbidden IP sites. If you're trying to reach one on that blacklist, the Chinese international-gateway servers will interrupt the transmission by sending an Internet "reset" command both to your computer and to the one you're trying to reach. Reset is a perfectly routine Internet function, which is used to repair connections that have become unsynchronized. But in this case it's equivalent to forcing the phones on each end of a conversation to hang up. Instead of the site you want, you usually see an on-screen message beginning, "The connection has been reset";

sometimes instead you get, "Site not found." Annoyingly, blogs hosted by the popular system Blogspot are on this IP blacklist. For a typical Google-type search, many of the links shown on the results page are from Wikipedia or one of these main blog sites. You will see these links when you search from inside China, but if you click on them, you won't get what you want.

The third barrier comes with what Lih calls "URL keyword block." The numerical Internet address you are trying to reach might not be on the blacklist. But if the words in its URL include forbidden terms, the connection will also be reset. (The Uniform Resource Locator is a site's address in plain English—say, www.microsoft.com—rather than its all-numeric IP address.) The site falungong.com appears to have no active content, but even if it did, Internet users in China would not be able to see it. The forbidden list contains words in English, Chinese, and other languages, and is frequently revised—"like, with the name of the latest town with a coal mine disaster," as Lih put it. Here the GFW's programming technique is not a reset command but a "black-hole loop," in which a request for a page is trapped in a sequence of delaying commands. These are the programming equivalent of the old saw about how to keep an idiot busy: Take a piece of paper and write "Please turn over" on each side. When the Firefox browser detects that it is in this kind of loop, it gives an error message that reads, "The server is redirecting the request for this address in a way that will never complete."

The final step involves the newest and most sophisticated part of the GFW: scanning the actual contents of each page—which stories *The New York Times* is featuring, what a China-related blog carries in its latest update—to judge its page-by-page acceptability. This again is done with mirrors. When you reach a favorite blog or news site and ask to see particular items, the requested pages come to you—and to the surveillance system at the same time. The GFW scanner checks the content of each item against its list of forbidden terms. If it finds something it doesn't like, it breaks the connection to the offending site and won't let you download anything further from it. The GFW then imposes a temporary blackout on further "IP1 to IP2" attempts—that is, efforts to establish communications between the user and the offending site. Usually the first time-out is for two minutes. If the user tries to reach the site during that time, a five-minute time-out might begin. On a third try, the time-out might be 30 minutes or an hour—and so on through an escalating sequence of punishments.

Users who try hard enough or often enough to reach the wrong sites might attract the attention of the authorities. At least in principle, Internet users in China must sign in with their real names whenever they go online, even in Internet cafés. When the surveillance system flags an IP address from which a lot of "bad" searches originate, the authorities have a good chance of knowing who is sitting at that machine.

All of this adds a note of unpredictability to each attempt to get news from outside China. One day you go to the NPR site and cruise around with no problem. The next time, NPR happens to have done a feature on Tibet. The GFW immobilizes the site. If you try to refresh the page or click through to a new story, you'll get nothing—and the time-out clock will start.

This approach is considered a subtler and more refined form of censorship, since big foreign sites no longer need to be blocked wholesale. In principle they're in trouble only when they cover the wrong things. Xiao Qiang, an expert on Chinese media at the University of California at Berkeley journalism school, told me that the authorities have recently begun applying this kind of filtering in reverse. As Chinese-speaking people outside the country, perhaps academics or exiled dissidents, look for data on Chinese sites—say, public-health figures or news about a local protest—the GFW computers can monitor what they're asking for and censor what they find.

Taken together, the components of the control system share several traits. They're constantly evolving and changing in their emphasis, as new surveillance techniques become practical and as words go on and off the sensitive list. They leave the Chinese Internet public unsure about where the off-limits line will be drawn on any given day. Andrew Lih points out that other countries that also censor Internet content—Singapore, for instance, or the United Arab Emirates—provide explanations whenever they do so. Someone who clicks on a pornographic or "anti-Islamic" site in the U.A.E. gets the following message, in Arabic and English: "We apologize the site you are attempting to visit has been blocked due to its content being inconsistent with the religious, cultural, political, and moral values of the United Arab Emirates." In China, the connection just times out. Is it your computer's problem? The firewall? Or maybe your local Internet provider, which has decided to do some filtering on its own? You don't know. "The unpredictability of the firewall actually makes it more effective," another Chinese software engineer told me. "It becomes much harder to know what the system is looking for, and you always have to be on guard."

There is one more similarity among the components of the firewall: They are all easy to thwart.

As a practical matter, anyone in China who wants to get around the firewall can choose between two well-known and dependable alternatives: the proxy server and the VPN. A proxy server is a way of connecting your computer inside China with another one somewhere else—or usually to a series of foreign computers, automatically passing signals along to conceal where they really come from. You initiate a Web request, and the proxy system takes over, sending it to a computer in America or Finland or Brazil. Eventually the system finds what you want and sends it back. The main drawback is that it makes Internet operations very, very slow. But because most proxies cost nothing to install and operate, this is the favorite of students and hackers in China.

A VPN, or virtual private network, is a faster, fancier, and more elegant way to achieve the same result. Essentially a VPN creates your own private, encrypted channel that runs alongside the normal Internet. From within China, a VPN connects you with an Internet server somewhere else. You pass your browsing and downloading requests to that American or Finnish or Japanese server, and it finds and sends back what you're looking for. The GFW doesn't stop you, because it can't read the encrypted messages you're sending. Every foreign business operating in China uses such a network.

VPNs are freely advertised in China, so individuals can sign up, too. I use one that costs $40 per year. (An expat in China thinks: *That's a little over a dime a day.* A Chinese factory worker thinks: *It's a week's take-home pay.* Even for a young academic, it's a couple days' work.)

As a technical matter, China could crack down on the proxies and VPNs whenever it pleased. Today the policy is: If a message comes through that the surveillance system cannot read because it's encrypted, let's wave it on through! Obviously the system's behavior could be reversed. But everyone I spoke with said that China simply could not afford to crack down that way. "Every bank, every foreign manufacturing company, every retailer, every software vendor needs VPNs to exist," a Chinese professor told me. "They would have to shut down the next day if asked to send their commercial information through the regular Chinese Internet and the Great Firewall." Closing down the free, easy-to-use proxy servers would create a milder version of the same problem. Encrypted e-mail, too, passes through the GFW without scrutiny, and users of many Web-based mail systems can establish a secure session simply by typing "https:" rather than the usual "http:" in a site's address—for instance, https://mail.google.com. To keep China in business, then, the government has to allow some exceptions to its control efforts—even knowing that many Chinese citizens will exploit the resulting loopholes.

Because the Chinese government can't plug every gap in the Great Firewall, many American observers have concluded that its larger efforts to control electronic discussion, and the democratization and grassroots organizing it might nurture, are ultimately doomed. An item on an influential American tech Web site had the headline "Chinese National Firewall Isn't All That Effective." In October 2007, *Wired* ran a story under the headline "The Great Firewall: China's Misguided—and Futile—Attempt to Control What Happens Online." Let's not stop to discuss why the vision of democracy-through-communications-technology is so convincing to so many Americans. (Samizdat, fax machines, and the Voice of America eventually helped bring down the Soviet system. Therefore proxy servers and online chat rooms must erode the power of the Chinese state. Right?) Instead, let me emphasize how unconvincing this vision is to most people who deal with China's system of extensive, if imperfect, Internet controls.

Think again of the real importance of the Great Firewall. Does the Chinese government really care if a citizen can look up the Tiananmen Square entry on Wikipedia? Of course not. Anyone who wants that information will get it—by using a proxy server or VPN, by e-mailing to a friend overseas, even by looking at the surprisingly broad array of foreign magazines that arrive, uncensored, in Chinese public libraries.

What the government cares about is making the quest for information just enough of a nuisance that people generally won't bother. Most Chinese people, like most Americans, are interested mainly in their own country. All around them is more information about China and things Chinese than they could possibly take in. The newsstands are bulging with papers and countless glossy magazines. The bookstores are big, well-stocked, and full of patrons, and so are the public libraries. Video stores, with pirated versions of anything. Lots of TV channels. And of course the Internet, where sites in Chinese and about China constantly proliferate. When this much is available inside the Great Firewall, why go to the expense and bother, or incur the possible risk, of trying to look outside?

All the technology employed by the Golden Shield, all the marvelous mirrors that help build the Great Firewall—these and other modern achievements matter mainly for an old-fashioned and pretechnological reason. By making the search for external information a nuisance, they drive Chinese people back to an environment in which familiar tools of social control come into play.

Chinese bloggers have learned that if they want to be read in China, they must operate within China, on the same side of the firewall as their potential audience. Sure, they could put up exactly the same information outside the Chinese mainland. But according to Rebecca MacKinnon, a former Beijing corre-spondent for CNN now at the Journalism and Media Studies Center of the University of Hong Kong, their readers won't make the effort to cross the GFW and find them. "If you want to have traction in China, you have to *be* in China," she told me. And being inside China means operating under the sweep-ing rules that govern all forms of media here: guidance from the authorities, the threat of financial ruin or time in jail, the unavoidable self-censorship as the cost of defiance sinks in.

Most blogs in China are hosted by big Internet companies.

Those companies know that the government will hold them responsible if a blogger says something bad. Thus the companies, for their own survival, are dragooned into service as auxiliary censors.

Large teams of paid government censors delete offensive comments and warn errant bloggers. (No official figures are available. Some outsiders say the censor workforce numbers in the tens of thousands; others, that those figures include many ordinary police and therefore wildly exaggerate the number of officials concentrating on the Internet.) Members of the public at large are encouraged to speak up when they see subversive material. The propaganda ministries send out frequent instructions about what can and cannot be discussed. In October 2007, the group Reporters Without Borders, based in Paris, released an astonishing report by a Chinese Internet technician writing under the pseudonym "Mr. Tao." He collected dozens of the messages he and other Internet operators had received from the central government. Here is just one, from the summer of 2006:

17 June 2006, 18:35
From: Chen Hua, deputy director of the Beijing Internet
    Information Administrative Bureau
Dear colleagues, the Internet has of late been full of articles and
messages about the death of a Shenzhen engineer, Hu Xinyu, as
a result of overwork. All sites must stop posting articles on this
subject, those that have already been posted about it must be
removed from the site and, finally, forums and blogs must
withdraw all articles and messages about this case.

"Domestic censorship is the real issue, and it is about social control, human surveillance, peer pressure, and self-censorship," Xiao Qiang says. Last fall, a team of computer scientists from the University of California at Davis and the University of New Mexico published an exhaustive technical analysis of the GFW's operation and of the ways it could be foiled. But they stressed a nontechnical factor: "The presence of censorship, even if easy to evade, promotes self-censorship."

It would be wrong to portray China as a tightly buttoned mind-control state. It is too wide-open in too many ways for that. "Most people in China feel freer than any Chinese people have been in the country's history, ever," a Chinese software engineer who earned a doctorate in the United States told me. "There has never been a space for any kind of discussion before, and the government is clever about continuing to expand space for anything that doesn't threaten its survival." But it would also be wrong to ignore the cumulative effect of topics people are not allowed to discuss. "Whether or not Americans supported George W. Bush, they could not *avoid* learning about Abu Ghraib," Rebecca MacKinnon says. In China, "the controls mean that whole topics inconvenient for the regime simply don't exist in public discussion." Most Chinese people remain wholly unaware of internationally noticed issues like, for instance, the controversy over the Three Gorges Dam.

Countless questions about today's China boil down to: How long can this go on? How long can the industrial growth continue before the natural environment is destroyed? How long can the superrich get richer, without the poor getting mad? And so on through a familiar list. The Great Firewall poses the question in another form: How long can the regime control what people are allowed to know, without the people caring enough to object? On current evidence, for quite a while.

CHINA'S SILVER LINING

JUNE 2008

Chinese cement plants and coal mines are grim enough taken separately. Often they come as a package, the plant built next to the mine to minimize transport costs for the vast quantities of coal the cement-making process consumes. Converting limestone and other materials to the intermediate form of cement called "clinker" requires heating them to more than 2,600°F. Getting kilns this hot requires burning about 400 pounds of coal for each ton of cement produced.

The clinker then cools before it goes through further processing—but the waste heat and exhaust gas are sent straight into the sky, at temperatures of 650°F or more, along with the extra carbon dioxide the limestone emits as it becomes cement.

In coal-and-cement towns in China, people and buildings are colored black by the coal dust swirling around them, and coated gray and white by the cement dust that leaks from the kilns and clinker coolers and pours from the exhaust stacks. Driving through the foothills of the Tibetan plateau in western Sichuan province last year, my wife and I could tell from miles away when we were nearing a cement plant, from the grayish pall in the air and the thickening layers of dust on the trees and road. With so much of the country under construction so fast, and with China's equivalent of America's interstate highway system being built in the space of a few years, modern China can appear to be made out of concrete. Nearly half of the world's cement is produced and used in China, and cement factories are a major source of both the country's surging demand for energy and the environmental damage that is the most shocking side effect of China's economic miracle.

Thus it was a surprise to drive toward a coal-cement complex in Zibo, a modest city of 4 or 5 million people in Shandong province, 230 miles southeast of Beijing, and see . . . no white haze. True, miners trudging along the street had blackened faces, and the city was dotted with 100-foot-high mounds of low-grade coal, previously trash but now worth picking over because of soaring world demand. But no white powder mixed with the black, and only wispy plumes of steam wafted from the fat, high smokestacks of the Sunnsy cement company (its name is from the Chinese *shansui*, or "mountain water"). Indeed, the fattest and somewhat rusty-looking central exhaust stack had been fitted with elaborate ductwork of obviously newer metal, which captured everything coming out of the stack and shunted it to a nearby new building.

Inside the new building was an electricity-generating plant, and what I was seeing was the handiwork of a Chinese engineer in his mid-forties named Tang Jinquan. Tang had never intended to get into the cement business. But when he graduated from the technical university in Harbin, in far northern China, the government was still assigning jobs to graduates—and his assignment was a cement-research institute in his hometown of Tianjin. "I am interested in heat generation, this place is about cement—no match!" he told me (through an interpreter) at the factory in Zibo. He spent nearly the next 20 years of his career in a long effort to make the dirty, wasteful, fast-growing cement industry less environmentally destructive.

The heart of his idea—easy to describe, tricky to implement—is capturing the enormous amount of heat normally wasted in cement making and using it to run turbines that generate electric power. This power can then be fed back into the factory, doing work that would otherwise require burning even more coal. The reduction of dust is a visible indicator of the more fundamental reduction of waste. Over the course of a long day, I heard about the many, many refinements Tang had made to this cogeneration system since he first started working on it in the mid-1980s. The punch line is that it now works well enough to cut the energy (mainly from coal) required to make clinker by 60 percent, and the overall power demands of the cement production line by 30 percent.

In 2004, Tang left the cement-research institute to form, with two colleagues, a technology start-up company called Dalian East Energy Development, which sells cogeneration systems to cement producers like Sunnsy. (It's a long way from the days of government-assigned jobs.) The energy-recycling system at the factory I saw is expected to cover its multimillion-dollar cost (the exact sum is confidential) within four years, through reduced coal demand and government rebates for energy-saving investments. Sunnsy is a private firm, with annual sales of more than $1 billion and a recent $50 million investment from Morgan Stanley. According to Tang, the 120 similar installations at cement factories throughout China save 1.7 million tons of coal per year.

When I met Tang, he had just returned from a trip to Vietnam, where two of his systems are operating, and was about to head to Uzbekistan, where he has another (others are in India, the Philippines, and Pakistan). His dream now is to apply his cogeneration technology to more of China's most wasteful industries, starting with steel. "I have a long vision, which may not be realized before I die," he told me when we had lunch. "Of course, that might not be so long!" he added, laughing and waving a cigarette at me—one of 60 he smokes per day.

Tang added that when he goes to class reunions from his university and sees that he is the only one in the cement business, "I feel unacceptable, because the industry is not good." But he says he knows otherwise, and he tells recruits to his firm to hold their heads high. "They should be proud of what we are doing! Other industries are consuming the earth. We are preserving it."

Here is what I learned by visiting the cement factory, and by seeing and asking about many similar "green" projects in China: China's environmental situation is disastrous. And it is improving. Everyone knows about the first part. The second part is important, too. Outside recognition of where and why China has made progress increases the prospects that it will make further advances. Recognition also clarifies the most important obstacles, political and economic, to such progress. And it is simply fair to the many people within China, including within the Chinese Communist Party, who are trying their best to make a difference—and who are having more success than most Westerners who rely on media accounts would suspect.

It is right, of course, that Western publications emphasize so often and so clearly the damage that China's economic rise has inflicted on its own environment and the world's. But the despairing tone of this coverage is itself becoming an issue within China—one more illustration in the long national narrative of not being fully appreciated or respected by the world's established powers. It might also be having an effect on what the government does.

Surprisingly enough, even official sources within China have gone far to recognize the challenges the country faces and its responsibility to deal with them. In November 2007, the Chinese government released its 11th Five-Year Plan for Environmental Protection. The tone of this document would come as a shock to anyone familiar with the relentlessly upbeat nature of official Chinese pronouncements—or with the famous mock-news video released by *The Onion* in spring 2008, in which Chinese authorities burst with pride as they announce their nation's new status as the No. 1 polluter in the world. (The mock festivities include the "100 Widow

Smog Dance" and a spokesman declaring, "The labor of the people has made the sky black with the smoke of progress. We are overjoyed!")

The "environmental situation is still grave in China though with some positive development," the real Chinese government said in the English translation it issued. It went on to catalog a familiar set of problems: "The emissions of major pollutants far exceed environmental capacity with serious environmental pollution. . . . The quality of coastal marine environment is at risk. . . . The number of days with haze in some big and medium-size cities has some increase, and acid rain pollution is not alleviated. . . . The phenomena of no strict observation of laws, little punishment to lawbreakers, poor law enforcement and supervision are still very common." And on through a very long list, with this stark conclusion: "China is facing [a] grim situation in addressing climate change. . . . Environmental problems at different stages of [the] industrialization process of developed countries over the past several hundred years [are now] concentrate[d] in China."

The alarming trends mentioned in this report correspond with what the outside world has heard, read, and assumed about the environmental disaster of modern China. A new book or white paper on the topic seems to appear every day. The surprise is seeing them acknowledged in a paper issued not by an international research group but by the Chinese government itself, which has long been accused of refusing to see what is plain to everyone else. The problems, after all, are visible to any tourist from the moment of arrival. Everyone has heard or read about China's big-city air pollution, yet visitors are still shocked the first time they encounter a bad day in Beijing—or Chongqing or Xi'an or Shenyang or any of the other large cities with chronically grimy skies.

And the problems that are less obvious at a glance are even more threatening. Toxic emissions into lakes, groundwater, and farmland; the drying-up of rivers and silting-up of dams; the rapid exhaustion of water in the northern half of the country that, in the view of many experts, is likely to be China's next great environmental emergency; the millions of new cars that hit the road each year, spewing carbon dioxide; the billions of tons of coal that go up in smoke (yes, billions—China burns more than 2 billion tons of coal each year, about one-third of the world's total); the engines on Chinese airliners that must be overhauled or replaced more frequently than elsewhere, an airline engineer told me, because operating in Chinese air corrodes the turbine blades . . . living here, I don't have the heart to keep ticking items off. The title of one authoritative book on the subject, *The River Runs Black,* by Elizabeth Economy of the Council on Foreign Relations, conveys the general idea, as does that of her follow-up *Foreign Affairs* article about China's environment, "The Great Leap Backward?"

Through nearly two years in China, including the winter and spring of 2008 in Beijing, my wife and I have found the bad air and other forms of pollution to be the only serious challenge—physical, practical, or emotional—we face. We are here temporarily and voluntarily, and we're living like royalty compared with most local Chinese. Still, we continually face a basic choice. Either we decide we can't stand the conditions, in which case we should leave—an option for most foreigners but few Chinese. Or we decide that the openness, possibility, and importance of today's China justify these and other discomforts, in which case we should stop complaining, try to ignore what we don't like, and be grateful for the historic opportunity we have. We keep deciding to stay. The point is, even privileged outsiders here must live with conditions they can't change, and those conditions are only a tiny window on the endurance required of the Chinese public.

But remember that other phrase from the government's 11th Five-Year Plan: there has been "some positive development" amid the catastrophe. After travels around the country to look at factories, farms, and conservation projects, and talks with several dozen scientists, think-tank experts, officials, and businesspeople from China and overseas, I have come to think that the modestly positive developments merit more of the world's attention than they've received.

There will be no shortage of attention for the next big test of China's environmental positive developments: the Beijing Olympic Games. In 2007, the economist Matthew Kahn ranked 72 major world cities on overall environmental "livability." Beijing came in dead last, below Bangkok and Mumbai. In 2001, as part of its agreement to host the Olympics, the Chinese government promised to bring the air quality up to the standards of previous Olympic venues—in addition to making other commitments about reducing press controls and increasing civil liberties for its people. Whatever the government might or might not do toward keeping the political commitments, most people assumed that it would take any steps necessary to make the air acceptable by the opening ceremony on August 8.

On a trip to Beijing in August 2006, I wondered when the authorities would ever get around to applying the clean-air plan. With each passing month, the woeful quality of Beijing's air and the implausible nature of official statements increased my skepticism that a normal Olympics could occur. At a press conference broadcast live from Beijing soon after I moved there from Shanghai, in October 2007, Jacques Rogge, the head of the International Olympic Committee, said that some events might have to be rescheduled unless things improved fast. My TV screen went black at that point, and his remarks were not covered in the local press. When the world-record holder in the marathon, Haile Gebrselassie of Ethiopia, said he wouldn't compete in that event for fear of hurting his lungs, the Chinese media pointed out that he hadn't yet been named to the team anyway. The Beijing city government was mocked in the foreign (though not the local) media for reporting an ever-improving count of "blue sky days" per month, which had to refer to something other than the actual color of the sky. I myself have been incredulous at the skies I see regularly outside the windows of the apartment my wife and I have been renting here. As a personal chronicle, I take a picture of the sky each day I'm in town, so I can record when, if ever, things really improve in preparation for the Games. (Current plans are to impose sweeping factory shutdowns and other emergency cleanup measures starting about three weeks before the Olympics begin.)

But, as at the cement plant, after I spent a day with the group of more than 20 scientists in charge of measuring the real quality of the city's air, I found myself less ready to scoff. These were physicists, atmospheric scientists, and other researchers from various institutes of the Chinese Academy of Sciences, or CAS. I met them at the Academy's Institute of Remote Sensing Applications, which is next door to the main Olympic site on the north side of Beijing.

The sky was a brilliant blue that day, thanks to the frigid wind roaring in from Mongolia. When the wind comes into Beijing from the west, as it did that day, it pushes the city's haze out toward the sea. But usually it comes from the south and southeast and brings smoke and dust from the hyper-polluted coal and steel regions of Shanxi and Shandong provinces, including the chokingly polluted coal city of Taiyuan, 250 miles southwest of Beijing. The smoke and dust from the south combine with Beijing's own automotive and factory fumes and hang over the city, trapped by mountains on the western edge. That's when the air is so dense and dark that spectators on one side of the Olympic Stadium will barely be able to see to the other.

I visited the scientists at a complex of about 15 research centers, plus an apartment block with housing for hundreds of CAS employees. The complex is next to the Olympic grounds, in an area where new public buildings of all sorts are going up. In a series of briefings and outdoor tours, the scientists laid out the steps they had taken to get honest measures of

Beijing's air problems. They built 1,000-foot-high towers in and around the city to measure pollutants at different altitudes and predict how the wind would spread them. They shot laser beams at reflectors on distant buildings and assessed the return signal to measure what was in the air. They mounted sensors on cars and vans and drove them around the city's ring roads to see where the pollution was worst. They converted the entire roof of their office building into an open-air lab overlooking the Olympic Village. American-made spectrometers measured particulates and pollutants like ozone and nitrous oxide. A satellite dish received a steady stream of data from U.S. geophysical satellites, which was then matched with their local findings. And that was just a start.

I couldn't judge the machinery, but everything about the people and process seemed serious and scientific rather than political. Therefore I was willing to listen when Liu Wenqing, the director of the Anhui Institute of Optics and Fine Mechanics, and Wang Yuesi, of the Institute of Atmospheric Physics, said that, according to the team's readings, the air in Beijing was actually improving. Between 2000 and 2006, the city's population went up by half, to 15 million, and in about the same time the number of vehicles on its roads doubled, to 3 million (apparently the scare stories about a thousand extra cars per day joining Beijing's traffic are true). But because of tougher auto-emissions standards that took effect in 2006— similar to America's CAFE rules, but more stringent—and the forced closing of many factories in and around the city, the levels of all major pollutants fell during the same period. (The pollutants included nitrous oxide, ozone, and VOCs, or volatile organic compounds, like benzene.) These were long-term changes, not whatever emergency shutdown measures the government will take just before the Games begin.

The last PowerPoint slide in a presentation that one of the scientists showed me read, "We are confident that the air quality goals for Olympics 2008 will be met in Beijing." When I asked, "Really?" all eyes turned toward the senior CAS official in the room, a British-trained scientist. "I personally am sure the goals will be met," he said. Even if the winds are wrong? "Ninety-nine percent."

I don't know whether he is right, but what I took from the day was that sophisticated people are honestly trying to do the right thing, in ways official propaganda had not prepared me for. Like England, the United States, Japan, and others before it, China is passing through the environmental-disaster stage of industrialization and beginning to clean up. The difference is that those countries waited until they were rich before they started the process. China is still full of poor people, but for reasons of scale and impact, it cannot postpone cleaning up.

There are signs that Chinese officials at many levels are facing that fact. An episode that seems to underscore China's stubbornness actually shows the reverse.

In 2004, the "Hu-Wen team" of President Hu Jintao and Premier Wen Jiabao had recently come into power with the slogan of building a "harmonious society." This specifically included greater harmony with nature. A man named Pan Yue, the deputy director of China's State Environmental Protection Administration, had been giving speeches about the need to measure the environmental cost of economic growth. (Pan, a former soldier and journalist now in his late forties— relatively young for an influential bureaucrat—has become the best-known spokesman for environmentalist causes in the government.) The agency, which in 2008 became the Ministry of Environmental Protection, approached the World Bank for help in conducting the first comprehensive survey of the total cost to the country, economic and otherwise, of China's air and water pollution.

"At first we were reluctant," a bank official who declined to be named told me. "These measures are always controversial and difficult"—especially any attempt to measure a toll in human lives. But there were signs that progressive elements inside the Chinese government wanted the study for use "as inside argument for devoting more effort to the environmental issue." The important background point is that even though the outside world tends to see China itself and "the Chinese regime" as a great homogenous bloc, there are ideological, regional, and personal rivalries at every level.

The economic calculations were sobering enough, to say nothing of the health consequences. When the World Bank issued its draft report, "Cost of Pollution in China," in the summer of 2007, it said that China's economic growth rate would be cut significantly—perhaps by half or more—if the government accounted realistically for what Pan Yue called the country's "overdrafts" on resources. China's announced growth rate has been 9 to 10 percent each year over the past two decades; the report said that environmental costs could represent between 2.9 and 5.8 percent, which would reduce

China's miraculous-seeming growth rate to sclerotic European levels. Estimating how many people were sick, dead, or deformed would of course be much more controversial.

According to widely reported leaks, the bank concluded that about 750,000 Chinese people die prematurely each year because of pollution. But the Chinese government requested that no total figure be included in an interim version of the report released in 2007, because it wanted to review the methodology behind the estimate. This move was blasted around the world as yet another sign of the government's secrecy.

The odd part of the denunciation is that the report itself, which the Chinese government accepted; included every bit of shocking information except that final tally. There were calculations of childhood deaths from dysentery, lost "life-years" because of air pollution, increased hospitalization rates because of lung diseases and cancers, and other grim statistics, including the conclusion that air pollution in all its forms is probably 10 times more damaging to China's health than all forms of water pollution. It is hard to imagine how anyone who opened the report could consider it a whitewash.

"The press reaction to the report really irritated us," the bank official said. "It's not just the Chinese—all governments we deal with are very careful with this kind of life-and-death data. All of us felt that the government was taking the exercise seriously and that it helped nobody to slap them down." Several people I spoke with at other international organizations concurred. Sure enough, in March 2008, after the hubbub had died down, a report on environmental policy by Xinhua, the state-run news agency, mentioned offhandedly that "a World Bank report said about 750,000 Chinese die earlier due to air pollution every year."

The Chinese Communist Party unquestionably rules China, but in a more haphazard and uneven fashion than Westerners often recognize. About some things it is as inflexible, intolerant, and oblivious to outside criticism as the worst stereotypes suggest. These hard-line areas include political challenges to the party's legitimacy, criticism in the media, and any suggestion of regional separatism or "splittism"—notably, uprisings in Tibet fomented by what the state-run media always refer to, in English, as the "Dalai clique." About many other matters, ranging from the daily practices of mayors or provincial governors to the deals struck by entrepreneurs, the central Communist government in Beijing is either unable to impose its will or uninterested in even trying. Economic development has been fastest in the parts of the country—mainly the south, far from Beijing—where the central government has been most hands-off.

The varied nature of the government's approach explains a theme I heard in many interviews. Both Chinese and foreign environmentalists said the government is sending subtle but important bureaucratic signals that it now takes environmental protection more seriously. It is more tolerant of Chinese and foreign nongovernmental organizations working for green causes. It is allowing more of its citizens a chance to defend their environmental rights via lawsuits or organized protests.

And it is changing the way it promotes and rewards its own officials, to move them toward an environmentalist outlook. There are still huge pressures in the opposite direction, like payoffs to mayors or governors from land developers. But the new signals are positive.

For example, until recently the curriculum at the Central Communist Party School, where future administrators are trained, included no environmental training whatsoever. In U.S. military terms, this was like the days when war colleges taught future generals nothing about counterinsurgency. That is now changing. I talked with two foreign representatives of nongovernmental organizations—Peggy Liu, of the Joint U.S.–China Cooperation on Clean Energy (JUCCCE), and Lila Buckley, of the Global Environmental Institute (GEI)—that have been working with the central and provincial party schools to develop new courses and emphases. Liu, a Chinese American veteran of the tech and venture-capital industries who now lives in Shanghai, started JUCCCE in 2007 as a way of pooling Chinese and international efforts on the environment (its name is pronounced "juice" in English and "*ju si*" in Chinese, meaning "coalition of thinkers"). The group is developing bilingual Web sites intended to connect Chinese scientists, officials, and bureaucrats with their counterparts overseas, and is trying to connect party officials and factory managers across the country with international advisers.

"This can be like the Human Genome Project," Liu said, referring to the way researchers around the world used the Internet to share the computational work of decoding the genome, thus completing the project in a decade rather than a century. So far, she said, the Chinese government has welcomed rather than impeded her projects. "The government's green policies are among the most progressive in the world—seriously," she told me. "The challenge is to build an environmentally conscious workforce and have it pervade at every level. It's as if Starbucks were building a whole coffee culture at once."

GEI, one of China's few homegrown, locally run environmental NGOs, also trains future government leaders. Chinese authorities keep such a careful eye on NGOs that the very concept of a "non"-governmental organization is peculiar in China—and all the more so since the tradition of civic action is so weak. Still, GEI has been free to conduct traditional conservation efforts such as supporting wildlife reserves; it has promoted wider adoption of energy-saving systems like the one used in the Sunnsy cement factory; and it has brought to the Tibetan hinterland simple, cheap "biogas converters" with which Tibetan villagers produce fuel for heating and cooking from yak or cattle dung. (What about the smell? Buckley, an American in her twenties who is GEI's only non-Chinese staff member, told me that the villages smell better with the converters than they did before, when the villagers burned the dried dung, and heaps of dung patties polluted their drinking water.)

And GEI has made a major push for a presence in party schools. This has required some delicate maneuvering, since the schools have naturally been slower than regular Chinese universities to bring in foreign experts. In 2006, GEI took two 12-member delegations of party instructors to the United States for three weeks of sustainable-development training at Stanford and Yale and for visits to the World Bank, Resources for the Future, and similar organizations.

By all accounts, the most important change in China's bureaucratic culture is revising the performance-rating system for officials so they are graded on environmental protection rather than mainly on economic growth. To explain the long-term significance this can have, it is useful to think of the professional U.S. military, which resembles China's nationwide Communist administrative system in this way: Ambitious young officers are rotated through a variety of command posts on their way to the top. In both, the organizational culture is continually reinforced through midcareer training—war college for future U.S. generals, party schools for future ministers and provincial governors. And career success depends heavily on performance evaluations at the end of each assignment that determine who moves up and who is sidetracked. Shifts in the rating system have a predictable and profound effect on individual behavior.

China's national laws about air and water pollution are also shifting in an environmentally responsible direction. In China even more than in the United States, law is one thing and reality is another—but in general, I was told, these pollution standards are being taken more seriously than they used to be. For instance, in spring 2008 a spokesman for the Shanghai Economic Committee announced the city's 20 goals for the year. Energy conservation and pollution control were at the top of the list.

"My sense is that local political leaders and the heads of big state-owned businesses understand that they really will be held accountable," Charles McElwee, an American environmental lawyer based in Shanghai, told me. The goals are quite explicit. For example, greater Shanghai is supposed to improve its "energy efficiency"—the amount of energy used per 10,000 RMB of economic output—by 4 percent each year. The nationwide goal is to increase energy efficiency by 20 percent and decrease emissions of major pollutants by 10 percent by 2010, compared with 2006 levels. That goal is theoretically still within reach, though 2007's achievements fell short (for instance, energy efficiency improved by 3.3 rather than 4 percent). In 2007, the reported level of COD—chemical oxygen demand, a major indicator of water pollution—went down by more than 3 percent nationwide, and the level of sulfur dioxide, a major air pollutant, by more than 4.6 percent. "When I saw those figures, it changed my perception of how things were headed in China," McElwee said.

In parallel with its own incentives on environmental issues, the government has warily tolerated forms of organized citizen action that it would usually restrict. Even as it has opened the country economically and socially, the government has tried hard to limit independent sources of information and any type of organization outside its control. Yet Greenpeace maintains programs and offices in China, where it has launched an aggressive (by Chinese standards) campaign to persuade consumers not to buy furniture made of rain-forest wood, not to eat shark-fin soup, not to waste energy—and not to buy products from Chinese or foreign companies that undermine these goals. Greenpeace China is quoted frequently in the press—yes, the Chinese press. Environmental exposés are increasingly tolerated, as political exposés are not, and they draw widespread attention.

The rule of law is still shaky in China, but Chinese environmental lawyers have filed and sometimes won suits on behalf of citizens who are sick because of pollution or whose farms have been poisoned. A former journalist named Ma Jun has created the remarkable online China Water Pollution Map for his Beijing-based group, the Institute of Public and Environmental Affairs. Anyone using the Internet can zoom in on a city or village, click on a lake or river, and see the latest pollution readings—and also which factories or farms are creating the problem. Jane Goodall's organization has started "Roots & Shoots" programs to teach Chinese children about environmental problems. In early 2008, thousands of people poured into the streets of Shanghai to protest the downtown extension of a Maglev train line, which they believed would give off dangerous radiation near their homes. There was a similar mass protest in 2007 about factory pollution in the coastal manufacturing town of Xiamen.

"China's greatest environmental achievement over the past decade has been the growth of environmental activism among the Chinese people," Elizabeth Economy, author of *The River Runs Black*, told me in an e-mail. "They have pushed the boundaries of environmental protection well beyond anything imaginable a decade ago."

How do we measure the good against the bad, the signs of progress against the devastated landscape and opaque skies? Here are three propositions to suggest, followed by one big challenge China poses to the world.

The first is simply that we acknowledge that the authors of the 11th Five-Year Plan were right. There are positive developments in China. And the situation is grave.

Renewable energy? More of it is coming online every day. Indeed, one of the world's leading producers of photovoltaic cells, Suntech Power, is based in Wuxi, near Shanghai. It is listed on the New York Stock Exchange, and its owner, Shi Zhengrong, is a billionaire. I have seen large windmill farms in Xinjiang province, where GE and Siemens compete to sell turbines. But because demand for power is increasing much faster than renewable supply, China burns about 10 percent more coal each year than it did the year before.

Automobiles? A similar picture. China recently adopted fuel-efficiency standards higher than those in the United States. But China now has only about one-twentieth as many cars per person as the United States does—about 35 million cars for 1.3 billion Chinese, versus 185 million cars for 300 million Americans. It will close that gap, and even though China's cars will become more efficient, there will be a lot, lot more of them. According to a recent analysis by the McKinsey Global Institute, China will have about 120 million vehicles by 2020. Outsiders, then, should give the Chinese credit for what they are achieving, without forgetting how much there is to do.

Second, the major problem with government policy in China is essentially the same one as in the United States: Despite the differences in political systems and overall wealth, both governments are afraid to make the public pay the true cost of cleaning up the country. And that could slow the process by many years.

What the United States has done for decades with oil and gasoline—namely, keep prices as low as possible, so its citizens can live the good life—the Chinese government has done with even more necessities. Gasoline is cheaper than in the United States, because the government subsidizes the refineries. Water, electricity, agricultural fertilizer, and above all coal—they all cost Chinese consumers less than their "real" cost to the country, in both environmental and economic terms.

"Just because a country is poor is not a reason to subsidize scarce goods," David Dollar, an American who directs the World Bank's China and Mongolia operations, told me in his office in Beijing. He explained the point this way: Some places in northern China and Mongolia use more water per capita than much of Europe, even though they're mostly desert and have nearly exhausted their aquifers. That's because they are allowed to pay so little for water. If people had to pay more, they would use less. "Chinese people," Dollar said, "tend to be very practical, if I may put it that way." The same is true of fertilizers. China's rivers and lakes are so foul in part because chemical fertilizers are subsidized. Farmers overuse them, and the runoff kills streams. If fertilizer cost more, farmers would use less, and less runoff would end up in streams. The Chinese government is planning a continental-scale system of canals to bring water from the south to the arid north. But over the next decades, Dollar argues, tens of millions of people are going to leave the northern farms for urban jobs in any case. It would be far saner—economically and environmentally—to scale back the canal-building and steer farms, factories, and people to the south, where the water is.

The urban version of this pattern involves electricity, gasoline, and public water supplies, all of them cheaper for consumers than their real cost to the country and the environment. Here, too, changes in price and policy can make large differences. For example, the Shanghai city government makes owning a car very expensive, and has relatively manageable traffic and excellent subways. The Beijing city government makes it cheap, and is being strangled and choked by cars.

"Underpriced energy is the world's largest subsidy for environmental destruction," William Chandler, of the Carnegie Endowment for International Peace, wrote in a report in spring 2008. "The Chinese government continues to intervene heavily in energy pricing, recently even freezing—in a profoundly wrongheaded move—key energy prices."

David Dollar is not Ebenezer Scrooge. The World Bank's recommendations for realistic prices include many schemes to offset the burden they would place on the country's impoverished majority. But he recognizes the trap the government is in. If China keeps these prices down, it will have even more trouble producing positive developments of any sort. If it lets them rise, it will face the anger of people for whom inflation is already the No. 1 domestic concern. Americans who reflect on their own experience with proposed hikes in gasoline taxes will recognize the difficulty of the choice.

The third proposition is more hopeful: The business of improving China's environment can be a very attractive business indeed. For corporations, it can mean profits, as with the newly efficient cement factories. For the world as a whole, it opens the possibility of a longer-term profit, in dealing with shared climate-change problems. Over the past 20 years, the world got used to a "China price" for manufactured goods— the rock-bottom price for anything coming out of a factory. In the coming 20 years, the world could make use of a "China price" for pollution control, especially greenhouse gases—the rock-bottom requirement of money and resources needed to reduce emissions by a given amount. Precisely because many Chinese systems are now so wasteful, it can be cheaper and easier to eliminate the next thousand tons of carbon-dioxide output or the demand for the next million watts of electricity-generating capacity here than anywhere else.

In late 2007 I went to Tsinghua University in Beijing, China's counterpart to MIT, to hear an American business-man address a group of young Chinese engineers. The visiting speaker was George David, the then CEO of United Technologies Corporation, and he had come to give a lecture that at first struck me as implausibly upbeat.

China consumes less energy per person than America, David said, because its people live so simply, and so many are on farms. But China's economy consumes much more energy per unit of economic output than America's—about four times as much, in fact—and that, he said, is good news. So is the fact that China's homes, schools, and office buildings are so wasteful in the ways they use energy for heating and cooling. China's traffic system suffers extreme congestion, which wastes more fuel. More good news! "The U.S. is tremendously inefficient, and China is worse," David said. "That is what gives us the opportunity"—both commercial opportunity for companies like his and strategic opportunity for groups fighting climate change worldwide.

He went on to make a point that became obvious once explained: Precisely because so much of the Chinese system is profligate and sloppy, the opportunity to improve efficiency, and cut back on pollution and energy use, is greater here than nearly anywhere else—and the savings can be achieved more cheaply. The energy wastefulness of China's economy affects the entire world because of the greenhouse gases it generates. And so as the world looks for ways to cut those emissions, China offers fast, easy, and inexpensive opportunities for improvement. For businesses, this means a market for efficient engines, sewage-treatment plants, solar cells and similar "clean" energy sources, and other technologies that help control pollution. For those working to control greenhouse-gas emissions, it means a fast, cheap way to make a difference.

David gave this illustration: Commercial and residential buildings are a deceptively important source of pollution and greenhouse-gas emissions. Worldwide, the energy needed to heat, cool, and illuminate buildings, together with the energy costs of putting them up and maintaining them, accounts for nearly 40 percent of total energy demand—even more than the energy used by all forms of transportation. Chinese office buildings and apartments are leakier than those in developed countries. They require about twice as much fuel to heat and cool as those in similar climates in Europe or North America, because many were built in the days when insulation was one of many unaffordable luxuries. Therefore, in principle it's cheap and easy to cut their power use: more insulation in existing buildings, higher standards for new ones.

Heating water by itself accounts for about 15 percent of the energy used in buildings. Switching to a different, technically proven means of heating water—"heat transfer" instead of "heat insertion"—would so dramatically improve efficiency that, according to David, it could lower total world energy demand by several percentage points.

Thus a corporate opportunity and an environmental opportunity coincide. Selling equipment and many other "green building" features to and within China will save money by cutting waste, plus modernize factories to reduce their energy use, too. For George David's arch-competitor, General Electric, that might mean selling windmill turbines to China; for his own UTC, it means selling elevators that, like hybrid cars, generate power whenever they brake and thus substantially cut total energy use. This in turn would have obvious benefits to the world. David and 10 CEOs from industrial companies in North America, Europe, and Japan have formed the World Business Council for Sustainable Development, which is pushing for similar innovations in urban design and building construction.

I saw one demonstration in a manufacturing zone an hour's drive west of Shanghai. A factory there will, when it becomes operational in a few months, produce a radically different sort of window glass for use in office buildings. The company, called Envision (and known as Vision Wall outside China), is based in Alberta, Canada, and uses a technique designed in the 1980s in Switzerland. It replaces the double-glazed windows normally used in apartments and offices with a complex structure that looks like a normal pane but has internal membranes and other devices that almost totally block the transmission of heat. These are the windows used at the U.S. National Science Foundation's research station at the South Pole, and they have been widely adopted in cold-climate buildings around the world—a government building in Minnesota, the airport in St. Louis, more than 500 installations in Canada and Europe. The company has a factory in Edmonton, Alberta, and another in Switzerland, where the equipment being installed near Shanghai was previously used.

At the factory, Albert Wong showed me the difference the windows could make. Wong, who is in his fifties, grew up in Shanghai and then studied chemistry at Louisiana State University, in Baton Rouge. (Time for a reminder: America's universities are *the* crucial connection between the U.S. and China.) He worked for Shell Oil and DuPont; he became a Canadian citizen; and in 2003 he returned to China to sell his windows. His company has taken infrared photos of Chinese buildings at night. The typical ones blaze red with radiating heat: Much of what comes into the building, from the furnaces, goes right out through the panes. (As I write this, I am sitting in a two-star Chinese hotel in the hinterland. It is cold and windy outside, and the breeze through the half-inch gap between the window glass and its frame ruffles the papers on the desk.) Then he showed me comparable photos of buildings with his windows. They are deep blue, the heat trapped inside.

These windows cost 10 percent more than standard glass. But if specified from the start, they can reduce construction costs for an entire building by 15 percent or more, since the heating and air-conditioning systems can be reduced by half. Plus, they save money each year on fuel.

The bad news is that not one of the windows is used in China yet. After five years of effort, Wong has yet to make a single sale here. The factory near Shanghai will supply customers in Korea, Japan, North America—but not the surrounding provinces. The barriers are the conservatism of the construction industry (not the most adventurous group in any country) and the fact that even if his windows save coal for China, they will cut out an existing glass manufacturer.

Many green businesses are already enjoying better luck, and Wong says that Envision is in China for the long haul. But his start-up difficulties illustrate the importance of helping Chinese factory owners, builders, and citizens realize the many opportunities for saving energy—and money—and reducing emissions that are open to them. "China has a golden opportunity to leapfrog old, inefficient technologies and introduce cutting-edge technologies at a relatively early stage of development," the McKinsey analysis said.

In one way or another, all the proposals for helping China make this new great leap forward do the same thing: apply money or other rewards or penalties to steer China in a greener direction, for instance, stricter requirements for the windows in office buildings. Many of the proposals involve a concept that the Bush administration has rejected but that Senators John McCain, Hillary Clinton, and Barack Obama all support: a world market in "carbon credits." When a million dollars spent on better building standards in China—or better smelters, or smokestack scrubbers, or any of a hundred other possibilities—could make a bigger difference in controlling world pollution than that same million dollars spent in the United States or France, there should be a way to make sure that million dollars gets spent in China.

W hen I was a child, it was incredible for my father to have even one cold beer," a man named Sean Wang, who works for Envision, told me recently. He grew up in Beijing in the 1970s. "Now people want twenty-four-hour heating, hot water, refrigerators. It is not sustainable unless we make a change." We met in a shiny and spectacular new office tower in central Beijing. In every direction around us in the city were construction and bustle. In every direction around us in the country were people moving from the villages, where they had a few flickering lightbulbs and a bicycle, to the city, where they expected elevators, cars, and espresso machines.

The conclusions I've suggested so far all bear on the ways that China's environment might be improving, however slowly, and whether and how that improvement might be sped up. All of these changes lead to one further and now unanswerable question that is raised by Sean Wang's comments. Promising as some trends might be, bright as is the potential for efficient, moneymaking green investments, does China's scale and ambition, plus its reliance on coal, simply doom the world's effort to control greenhouse-gas emissions?

China is no idle bystander to this discussion. Its major rivers originate in glaciers on the Tibetan plateau, which have begun to melt. Even if every building in China were to be better insulated and built with Albert Wong's windows, and every factory were equipped with Tang Jinquan's cogeneration pipes, would China's newfound commitment be coming too late? One data point among hundreds: A recent study by Maximilian Auffhammer and Richard Carson, of the University of California, concluded that without some startling change in technology, China cannot avoid increasing its greenhouse-gas emissions faster than other countries can possibly cut theirs back.

Startling changes in technology have appeared over the past century. Antibiotics, to name the one that has made the biggest difference in human welfare. Telecommunications, from the radio to the Internet. Air travel and knowing our world from space. Startling changes in energy technology are now necessary—in producing, conserving, and containing the by-products of fossil-fuel combustion. This is the next big technological challenge for the world as a whole.

The world will have more time to work toward a solution if it nurtures promising developments in China—and if it recognizes that its most populous nation is doing some things right.

HOW THE WEST WAS WIRED

OCTOBER 2008

You could compare the far west of China to America's western frontier, if U.S. territory reached only to Nevada. In China as in the United States, when you head west into the continent from the crowded eastern urban corridor, the land becomes drier, the trees are sparser and the cities farther apart, and eventually you're in stark desert. But in China there is no coastline with fish and forests on the other end. Just more desert, steppe, and mountain, until the country reaches its borders with "the 'Stans"—Kazakhstan, Kyrgyzstan, and the rest.

In China's history, some interior cities have been prosperous and powerful, especially when the Silk Road trade routes to the Middle East and Europe brought commerce through places like Dunhuang and Xi'An. But in modern times, to say *xi bu* ("the west") in China is to signify the poorest part of the country, as "the South" meant in America for a hundred years after the Civil War.

Only a quarter of China's population lives in the western provinces and "autonomous regions," including Tibet. But that is more than 300 million people, roughly the entire population of the United States, many of them trapped in a kind of subsistence economy hard to imagine from the perspective of even China's own major eastern cities. After trips to a number of these areas—Gansu, Ningxia, Qinghai, Xinjiang, the western parts of Sichuan and Shaanxi—I was sobered as I have been by nothing else in the country.

If I were running a travel agency, I would skip the likes of Beijing and Shanghai and send foreign visitors out toward these western villages, where they would see aspects of China beyond its urban spectacle and manufacturing prowess. In China's most famous cities, tourists are surprised by the scale, speed, intensity, and ambition of the activity all around them. But seeing all this firsthand mainly gives a more detailed confirmation of the impression they already had. Even the poverty of the big cities, impossible to ignore and startling because it appears right next to the fanciest luxury projects, involves people who are connected to the modern world: For instance, migrant construction workers live oppressed and very dangerous lives, but they work on fancy high-rise office buildings and new freeway overpasses.

But in the villages, people effectively live in a different century. Their families may exist on the cash equivalent of $10 or $15 per month. Their entire life experience may be encompassed within a radius of ten or twenty miles. When my wife and I visited a high school in an ethnic Tibetan village in Gansu province, we were the first foreigners the students—or any of their teachers, or the principal—had ever seen outside of textbooks. At that school and others in the west, we talked with children who went to school in some years and didn't in others, depending on whether their families had sold enough crops to pay the public-school fees. This is not the China most foreigners read about or experience on visits, but its isolation and poverty are important parts of any understanding of China.

To my taste, the arid western provinces are the most beautiful parts of China. The eastern seaboard is mainly flat, featureless, overdeveloped, and devastated. Much of the west is awe-inspiring to see. This is the austere beauty of the desert: limitless vistas, clear skies, dramatic topography, an unforgiving environment for life of any kind.

Several of the trips we took through western villages were in the company of a Taiwanese-born software expert in his early sixties named Kenny Lin, who is now engaged in the most touching and quixotic enterprise I have seen in China— one that my wife and I felt moved to support after seeing its effects in rural schools. During the year I've followed Lin, I've found his efforts both fascinating and significant, in this sense: They underscore the depth of the economic challenges today's mighty China still faces. And they suggest the power of a new way of dealing with those challenges. This involves neither the government edicts that have guided the economy for decades nor the me-first capitalist vigor of recent years, but instead a deliberate use of market incentives and technological tools in what Kenny Lin calls an altruistic way.

To see what this means in 2008 requires going back more than forty years, to Lin's friendship in Taiwan with his college classmate Sayling Wen.

In the summer of 1966, Lin and Wen started college in the electrical-engineering department of National Taiwan University, in Taipei. Lin's father was a doctor and politician; Wen's, an electrician who died when his son was young. Wen was smart and the most diligent among his group of friends. After graduation in 1970 and mandatory military service, he joined one of the small electronics companies then proliferating in Taiwan. Over the next quarter century, he grew very rich, as Taiwan went through an outsourcing and manufacturing boom like the one that recently got under way in mainland China.

As the mainland Chinese economy opened in the 1990s, business opportunities, plus his own curiosity, led Wen to spend more and more time on the mainland. In 1992 his company, Inventec, built its first mainland factory, in Shanghai. Wen had long been a man of passions and pet projects. For instance, from the start of his career, he was convinced that the right English-teaching software could make it easy for Chinese speakers to learn English and, in his view, end their isolation from world discourse. (So far, no dice.) In 2000, he developed a new and very powerful passion: to save the poor people of western China.

Through the 1990s, Wen had traveled incessantly through China's industrial areas. In the summer of 2000, he had his first exposure to the driest and perhaps most challenging of the western regions: Gansu province, in the windblown yellow-earth plateau on the edge of the Gobi Desert. At an economic conference in Gansu's capital, Lanzhou, he heard officials compare China's development of its western frontier to the development of the American West, a process that would unfold over many generations.

Wen strongly disagreed. He stood up to say that even a 50-year target was unacceptable. For one thing, it was too far off to fit into any business's investment plans. With the advantages of airplanes, telecommunications, and global trade, progress should be much faster. Moreover, the 300 million people living in the arid west were "like us, all children of the Yellow Emperor, sharing the same ancestral blood," yet still living in poverty. If China let them languish another fifty years, "their suffering would be unbearable."

He had a new idea: Western China would have to become fully modernized—brought into parity with Shanghai and Beijing—within ten years, by 2010. Soon he had written a manifesto called "Develop Western China in Ten Years," which was published in English and Chinese, and he steered Inventec's money toward sites in the west. And he learned that he would have an unexpected ally: his old classmate Kenny Lin.

In the years after college in Taipei, Kenny Lin went to the United States, earned a doctorate, and had a successful twenty-year run as an engineer, researcher, and manager, winding up at Bell Labs and NYNEX. He married a woman from Taiwan, became a U.S. citizen, and raised two children. But China's opening under Deng Xiaoping attracted him, and after investigating various possibilities, he left the United

States and in 1993 started a software center in Tianjin, out-side Beijing, for his friend Sayling Wen's Inventec company.

One of Lin's engineers in the Tianjin software facility, Peng Haina, had spent a year as a volunteer teacher in a remote, desolate village in Gansu province called Huang Yang Chuan, literally "Yellow Sheep River." It lay at the junction of two shallow streams in a gorge eight thousand feet above sea level. The village of several thousand people had two streets. Most families lived in mud-brick-walled courtyard structures where their sheep and cattle also slept. In the frigid high-altitude winter, they kept warm by burning charcoal or animal dung inside their homes, in the lower part of large rectangular brick structures called kangs. They sat and slept on top.

Economically they survived by grazing sheep on already overgrazed, dry, and rapidly eroding hillsides, and by grow-ing wheat and potatoes when there was enough rain. The people of Yellow Sheep River had virtually no contact with the world beyond their little gorge, except when young men and women who had fled hundreds of miles to take factory jobs returned for a few days each year during the Chinese New Year holiday to see their hometown, and often the chil-dren they had left behind. Peng encouraged his Inventec col-leagues to donate books and computer equipment to the school and told Lin that he, too, should visit western China, which he had never seen. In late September 2000, Lin went to Yellow Sheep River and afterward decided to change the direction of his life.

In a book recounting that visit, which he wrote during a two-week burst, Lin described the hardships of the life he had seen in the hinterland—and also a solution that had come to him. It was a solution in the same spirit that had already motivated his old classmate Wen, though at the time he had no idea of Wen's own interests.

The hardship that stunned him most was the powerlessness of rural people against brute natural misfortune. A bright and promising young girl had made it through elementary school—but then a drought dried up the crops, and her peasant parents pulled her out of school because they didn't have money for the fees. In an hour-long video documentary he made to accompany the book (available at YellowSheep River.com), Lin showed the peasant parents saying they mainly wanted to get the girl married off as soon as possible. (An uncle then gave her money for school.) Another boy was shown sobbing about the dim fate that awaited his younger sister, who had been pulled out of elementary school to save money and would remain uneducated like their parents. "Oh God, help these simple and innocent children out of the poverty, deliver them from the tortures of the lack of rain," Lin wrote.

Lin's immediate impulse was direct charity. On his first visit, he pledged 2,500 RMB per month, about $365, to pay for meat in the school lunches and for fuel to boil drinking water. But he believed in "teach a man to fish"–type help rather than long-term charity, and so he conceived his scheme.

The villagers' fundamental problem was their isolation. The Internet could solve that! Lin's branch of Inventec could give more computers and software to the school. It could work with the local government to bring in a broadband line and set up a computer center that everyone in the village could use. The students could take courses far beyond the range offered by their impoverished school. They could communicate with people they had not known all their lives. The local farmers could use the Internet to learn about the weather and market conditions. Local craftsmen could offer items for sale to distant customers. Working-age people could look for good factory jobs elsewhere. "The shackles that had bound their spirits had been taken off," Lin wrote after he had, within a few weeks of his first visit (things happen fast in China), established the computer center, declared Yellow Sheep River an "Internet village," and created the Yellow Sheep River Web site.

It was just after his momentous first trip into the mountains that Lin saw Sayling Wen again. The year 2000 was the thirtieth anniversary of their college graduation, and Wen sent a note to his classmates saying that he was now so rich, he'd throw a celebration in Shanghai for the entire class and their families at Christmastime and pay their way. (His choice of Shanghai for a reunion of Taiwanese alums is an indication of the near-total integration of the mainland and Taiwanese economies.) On Christmas Day, he overheard Kenny Lin say that Yellow Sheep River now gave purpose to his life. Neither man had known about the other's recent interest in western China. Both had converted to Christianity, and both thought of helping western China partly as a spiritual obligation.

Wen told Lin about his vision of parity with the big cities within ten years for these destitute areas and said that the

"Internet village" was the model he had been looking for, since it could leapfrog the long process of industrialization and bring villagers directly into the telecommunications age.

Very soon, Wen had founded and funded a new company and put Lin in charge. Its name in English is "Town and Talent Technologies." Everything about it reflected Wen's love for the grand gesture. Had Lin brought the Internet to one village? It should come to a thousand villages. Might it cost $50,000 to equip, operate, and maintain each village's new computer center? Then Wen should commit $50 million, to cover all thousand villages.

Plus an extra $4 million, for what Wen saw as the crowning touch: a five-star luxury conference center in Yellow Sheep River itself, kind of an Aspen or Jackson Hole without the surrounding rich people. There Chinese visitors from the rich eastern cities could see how their countrymen lived, and so could visitors from around the world. Wen kept adding new specs and features to the resort. A conference room with special acoustic tile and high-end video projectors. A swimming pool with the latest "antiwave" design to prevent needless ripples, plus a gym. Naturally, broadband in all the rooms.

Wen used his connections and pull to interest governmental and industrial groups in the project, and he kept encouraging and funding Lin's work. Then he dropped dead.

In December 2003, as Town and Talent was setting up Internet projects at more than fifty western schools and as the external structure of the resort was being finished, Sayling

Wen suddenly suffered a stroke. He'd always been over-weight—standing behind him in line for mandatory fitness training back in their first week of college, Kenny Lin had been startled to see Wen weigh in at 99 kilos, 218 pounds, and strain valiantly but be unable to complete a single pull-up. (Lin, in contrast, was and is a physical-fitness fanatic.) But Wen had seemed vigorous and healthy. He was taken to the hospital and within three days had died, at age fifty-five.

Kenny Lin was devastated for his friend, and he was also in trouble. Wen had given him only $1.2 million of the promised $4 million total for the resort. "I had 400 construction workers ready to start on the interior," he told me. "No one knew where the other $2.8 million was." Wen had apparently told no one else in the company about his commitment. Lin stalled the workers, telling them that the hotel might become a school. He feared a riot if they knew that the whole project was at risk. Finally, in March 2004, after three months of Lin's pressure and pleading, one of Sayling Wen's brothers agreed to provide the missing $2.8 million.

By the end of 2004 the conference center was done, and officials from around China attended a grand-opening cere-mony. "But our original business model was lots of confer-ences, and Mr. Wen, with his connections, was the central part of that model," Kenny Lin told me. "Now there is no one to invite the people he could bring."

Lin told me this in the summer of 2007, as my wife and I walked along the echoing marble floors of the conference center, beneath a larger-than-life-size portrait of Sayling Wen on the wall. We had heard about Yellow Sheep River, which has been well publicized in China, and we had gotten in touch with Lin through mutual friends. In the 145-room resort, we appeared to be the only paying guests (the list price is about $100 a night). A full, uniformed staff was on hand— to welcome us to the breakfast buffet, to hand us towels at the pool and exercise room, to greet us when we went in and out the front door.

I have seen deserted resort-palaces before—for example, a ghostly one in the Ilocos area of northern Luzon, which Ferdinand Marcos had built strictly for his daughter's wedding and which stayed open, empty, for years after he was deposed. But this was different, in retaining an air of hopefulness rather than sheer decadence. And hopeful is how I feel about the several legacies of Sayling Wen's vision for western China.

The resort itself is of course the most visible of these legacies. When I run my travel agency, I will send every foreign group there I can. By international standards, it is no longer superluxurious. But for foreigners it is comfortable, which cannot be said of many other places where outsiders are a two-minute walk away from village life. Unlike similar "comfortable" lodgings in places like Haiti or West Africa, it creates little sense of surviving behind barricades in a gilded cage. The hotel and conference center are in the middle of ordinary peasant fields but not besieged by desperate local crowds. As in much of China, including some areas of the west, my wife and I walked through the region chatting with farmers and children in basic Mandarin without causing too much stir.

Kenny Lin, who turned over management of the resort to a colleague in 2005, was aiming for a high-end international crowd of visitors. He knew that the surrounding mountainous area would appeal to Western hikers, mountain bikers, and horse riders. The highland scenery is breathtaking, like Wyoming or the Canadian Rockies, with numerous white yaks in place of bison or bears. (Breathtaking literally, too. While my wife rode horses among the yaks with Lin, I foolishly attempted to run along a path in the same meadow, only to stop in my tracks ten seconds later. It turns out that the meadow is at an elevation of 11,000 feet.) The resort's new manager has decided that the domestic Chinese tourist and conference business, a very rapidly growing market, offers the best prospects, and reportedly has booked enough of them to keep the business running.

A second legacy of Sayling Wen is the Town and Talent company, with its plan to bring the power of the Internet to isolated villages. The strategy behind that plan has also changed significantly since Lin's first trip to Yellow Sheep River eight years ago. Then, he thought the Internet could best help the young people of Gansu by helping them move away. They could learn what they needed to know to take factory jobs, and then be matched with big employers in the big cities. "Outsourcing labor to factories was a big economic success," Lin says, "but ethically, we couldn't be responsible for what happened to the kids. They were country children. They didn't know how to handle money in the big cities. They didn't know how to make friends or even cross streets."

Now Town and Talent's strategy is the reverse. It still wants to help children leave subsistence farms, on land that was barely farmable even before the drought and has been overused to the point of exhaustion. But instead of speeding their departure to the east and further straining family and social ties, it is trying to use the Internet to create new jobs in western China's cities. To oversimplify, the plan has similarities to India's success in creating call-center and tech-support jobs in Bangalore and Hyderabad, except here the idea is to attract jobs that might otherwise end up in Shanghai, Hangzhou, or some other booming eastern Chinese city. Town and Talent has set up programs in more than 150 schools in western China to train students in using computers (which it donates) and the Internet, so they will have a better chance of holding tech jobs or starting companies of their own.

The final legacy is outright philanthropy, the current version of Sayling Wen's obviously impossible dream of modernizing the west within ten years. The Town and Talent company devotes 10 percent of its efforts to a project whose English name is "West China Story" and whose goal is to connect students in remote villages with the outside world.

In this program, middle school and high school students in distant areas apply for a kind of work study grant. The standard amount, about $115, covers most of their yearly school expenses and so can keep them enrolled even when times are bad. (In many of the schools I've seen, the students sleep in cramped concrete dorm rooms on weeknights, because their homes are too far away for daily travel by bus or on foot. Part of the fee is to cover their food at school.) In exchange they must, essentially, become bloggers. At least ten times per year, they are required to research, write, illustrate, and post on the Web a report on some aspect of their lives in the countryside. The idea is to remind them that they are earning their way, not being given a favor, while at the same time teaching them modern Web site design skills. In addition, teams of students put up elaborate multipage Web sites—on the prospects for wind turbines in perpetually gusty western areas, on the history of irrigation systems in the Yellow River basin of Ningxia—some of which have won prizes in international high school "cyber-fairs."

The essays are available at WestChinaStory.com; they are in Chinese, but the students correspond with site visitors in simple English as part of their training. Many of the pictures are eloquent, regardless of language. (Town and Talent gives each school one digital camera, which the students share.) One middle school student writes about the "moment of joy" when the family wheat crop is ready for harvest. A high school boy tells about how great it was when his school got a basketball to play with outside. Another, about learning Tibetan dance. Another, what is hard but satisfying about herding sheep. It might sound maudlin, but having met some of these children, I take their accounts as alive, hopeful, human.

Some 2,200 rural students now earn their keep through this kind of blogging, supported by half a million dollars in donations mainly from Taiwan, Hong Kong, the United States, and a few businesses in mainland China. My wife and I signed up to "hire" a number of blogging students from the school that welcomed us. (On the site, you can not only see all of the students' essays in Chinese and their pictures but also choose students to sponsor at 800 RMB, or about $115, per year.) I'd like to know what becomes of them.

"The children in these villages have so many disadvantages," Ted Wen, Sayling's son, told me when I met him in Taipei. "They do not have a fair chance." For instance: Chinese universities reverse the logic of U.S. affirmative action programs. Rich and poor students alike take the gaokao, the nationwide admissions test. But to get into the famous, career-making universities, a poor student from the hinterland must score higher than a rich kid from an elite urban school. (This is the practical effect of a system whose stated bias is in favor of students from each university's own geographical area, and where the best universities are in the biggest, richest cities.)

Ted Wen is a suave figure in his early thirties who studied computer science in Japan and California before returning to Taiwan after his father's death to "get involved in my father's unfinished business," as he wrote to me in an e-mail. He said that his father's vision for western China was in part purely practical: If Taiwanese businesses did good things for mainland China, maybe people on the mainland would look favorably on Taiwan. But it also had a moral core. "I think it was important to my father to give children in the west a fairer chance to compete."

That effort might be doomed. The children might still have no hope. The west of China may still be poor ten years from now, and a hundred. But in a big, bustling country where many people are thinking mainly about what's profitable, it's worth noticing the ones who are thinking about what's fair.

AFTER THE EARTHQUAKE

Chinese officials and most of the Chinese public assumed that the year 2008 would be a major turning point for the country. They were right, but not for the reason they expected. Before the year began, expectations naturally focused on the Beijing Olympics, to be held in August. For all of the pageantry, expense, and overall success of the Olympic Games, the more important event of the year was the catastrophic earthquake in Sichuan province that occurred on May 12, followed by hundreds of aftershocks that themselves would count as major earthquakes in most countries.

The Wenchuan earthquake, as it was generally known in China after the small city where it was centered, may have killed 100,000 people directly and put many millions out of their homes. For more than two months, until the opening of the Olympics, reaction to the earthquake eclipsed other concerns in China. The date 5/12 on posters and magazine covers became as ubiquitous and significant as 9/11 had been in the United States. What had previously seemed an urgent national problem—the disruptions and protests as the Olympic torch relay moved through Western countries—virtually disappeared from the news.

The emergency changed China's internal sense of charity and mutual help. Volunteers took buses and trains from the big eastern cities toward Sichuan to volunteer to help. China does not have a long tradition of philanthropy, but donation boxes appeared everywhere—in office buildings, on street corners, in grocery stores—and were stuffed with RMB bills. It also changed the outside world's view. As a means of showing China's "true face" to the world, the unplanned and heartfelt response from Chinese citizens and institutions did more good than the carefully choreographed effort to astonish world viewers during the Games.

The crisis even portrayed the government in a positive light. China rapidly opened itself to international assistance, in unmistakable contrast to the shocking indifference of the Burmese junta at the same time. Nothing involving Chinese media treatment of a Chinese leader is ever unscripted. But Premier Wen Jiabao came close to an appearance of spontaneity in the weeks after the earthquake—flying to Sichuan within hours of the first news; slipping in the mud as he walked through the ruins; lecturing soldiers and rescue workers on the need to keep trying as long as there was the slightest chance that even one more survivor could be saved.

Ten weeks after the quake, in early August, when the nation's attention had shifted back to the impending Olympics, my wife and I traveled for a week through villages around the earthquake zone in western Sichuan. We were in the company of outsiders with long experience in this area, two scholars from the United States who had lived with Sichuan farmers and continually revisited them starting in 1992.

John Flower and his wife, Pamela Leonard, in their late forties, had immersed themselves so deeply in the life of western Sichuan that their fluent spoken Chinese attracted attention in other parts of the country because of its distinct regional accent. It was as if academics from Sweden had studied southern Louisiana so deeply that they sounded like Cajuns when they spoke English. Just before we met, Flower had left a tenured position as a history professor at the University of North Carolina–Charlotte to direct the extensive Chinese studies program at Sidwell Friends School, in Washington. Leonard, who had been an active farmer and anthropologist specializing in rural development, was now mainly raising their five-year-old son, Jack. The little boy, a towhead who also spoke Sichuan-accented Chinese and practiced skillful-looking kung fu moves whenever he was bored by the adults' discussion, was probably photographed 1,000 times by fascinated Chinese onlookers during the week we traveled with him.

We accompanied the family on their regular route of visits to Sichuan villages where they were well-known and warmly greeted returning figures. Day by day this course took us closer and closer to the center of the earthquake damage.

From the start, the landscape itself revealed the enormity of what had occurred. The mountains of Sichuan are so steep that their North American counterparts could be found only in Alaska. The slopes rise out of river valleys at what look like impossibly sharp angles to elevations of 12,000 feet and more. Usually they are covered in green, especially bamboo. But for more than 100 miles in all directions from the center of the earthquake, the hillsides displayed broad brown gashes, where entire sides of mountains had simply fallen away. Seeing them, I finally could envision how villages had disappeared all at once. They had been engulfed in rock and dirt, as mountain cabins are covered by snow in an avalanche. In the first few days, we saw villages that had escaped such burial and where at most tiles had been shaken off roofs or cement foundations cracked. By the end we saw areas where barely any structures were left.

The course of this journey also revealed a more surprising sequence, which had to do with the highly variable roles of the Chinese state.

Outsiders often discuss the Chinese state—that is, China's political and governmental system—and the Chinese nation as if they were the same entity. That is the way the Chinese government would prefer it: that the Chinese Communist Party be seen as the vessel of modern China's independence and of ancient China's culture, too. The elaborately wrought Olympic opening ceremony was essentially a dramatization of this view. It was meant to trace the unbroken line from imperial China, with its innovations in calligraphy and early science, to today's hyperproductive system that can do anything, including winning gold medals, on an unmatched scale.

Academics inside and outside China naturally take a more complicated view of the role and power of the state. One standard remark is that today's China, like all its predecessors, is "a civilization pretending to be a nation-state." That is, a billion-plus people in mainland China, plus the vast diaspora of overseas Chinese, share strong traditions and some sense of connection. The connection is often felt and sometimes expressed in simple racial terms. Recently I met a Beijing-born woman who now held a U.S. passport. She was trying to get into a Chinese government facility closed to all foreigners. The guard looked at her passport and said, "But you're still Chinese, right?" and let her in. Yet now, as in most stages of Chinese history, the political system that attempts to govern the sprawl and diversity of China is not fully in control.

In practice, most foreigners encounter this division as an either/or matter. As mentioned in earlier chapters, today's China is a disorienting combination of the very tightly controlled and the seemingly out-of-control. If you are interested in challenging the Communist Party's monopoly on power or even creating any organization not subject to state control, you will have problems. If you want to start a new electronics firm or perhaps a for-profit business school, no one in authority will care. Previous chapters have described the parts of Chinese policy where central government decisions are the only things that matter—setting the value of the yuan, determining who can see what on the Internet—and areas where the government is mainly hands-off. In the export-factory zones around Shenzhen, the most visible role of the government is to keep the ports and highways functioning so outbound FedEx and UPS shipments are never delayed.

Outsiders sometimes mention, almost as a footnote, that

decisions or goals announced in Beijing can mutate into something quite different when put into effect at the provincial or village level. Usually this is meant as a bad thing, mere sand in the gears, for instance when sweetheart deals between mayors and industrial tycoons prevent environmental cleanups.

I looked at local government in a different way after seeing these villages in Sichuan. Not from the opposite perspective—that local government is always wisest, commissars in Beijing are out of touch—but with a more sober appreciation of how hard and complicated it is to get anything done in China. Here are brief scenes from four of them.

XIAKOU: THE GOOD LIFE

The village of Xiakou was the closest thing the Flower-Leonard family had to a home in China. In 1992 and 1993, and for many summers since, they lived with the Wu family in a normal rural house without plumbing, running water, or heat except what emanated from the cooking fire. The area is at high elevation and has heavy winter snows. How do people stay warm? I asked Flower. "They wear a lot of clothes."

The village is now a success story, but of a different sort from the stories of prosperity through industrialization I had heard in many other parts of China. Fifty years ago, Xiakou, like much of rural China, suffered true catastrophe. In 1958, Mao Zedong introduced his new plan for China to "leap" ahead in industrial production by shifting millions of workers away from the farms and onto doomed projects like small-scale neighborhood steel mills. This was the "Great Leap Forward," or the "Great Famine," as it was known in the countryside. The theory was that China would overtake Great Britain in steel output within five years. The reality was that food production plunged and unknown millions of people starved.

Yao Minggao, the patriarch of another local family Flower and Leonard have stayed close to, was a young father at the time. Half the people in his village died. Bad national policy became even more brutal, or slightly less destructive, on a village-by-village basis, depending on the rigidity or flexibility of the commissar applying each new dictate from the party. The more doctrinaire the local leader, the more grain he was likely to seize from farmers in his area for "collective" purposes, and the less he left them to eat. John Flower pointed out to me that from the village center alongside a river, the steep hillsides where farmers grew crops were all within view. The commissar would scan the hills for wisps of smoke, so he could see who was starting an unauthorized fire and cooking food they had somehow found.

Yao Minggao, the family elder, said that the easiest way to tell city people from country people was by what they thought was the major disaster in modern Chinese history. If they said the Cultural Revolution, it meant they were from the city and viewed losing their careers and being sent to the farms as the ultimate hardship. If they said the Great Famine, it meant they were country people who had seen many of their neighbors starve.

In the 1960s, the collective-farm plots around Xiakou became productive again. When the fields were privatized in the 1980s, output soared. But more intensive and profitable agriculture soon created its own complications. Starting in the river valleys, farmers clear-cut their way up the steep mountainsides, planting corn and wheat in narrow terraces they had hacked out of previously forested area. These mountains in Sichuan were part of the wild habitat of the giant panda, and terraced agriculture dramatically shrank the pandas' range. Without tree cover, the torrential Sichuan rains caused severe erosion. In 1998, the uncontrolled runoff led to floods of the Yangtze River, which killed some 2,000 people.

In response, the central government issued perhaps its first significant environmental edict: the "grain to green" plan, *tuigeng huanlin* in Chinese, under which farmers would be paid to replace the terraced plots on hillsides with stands of bamboo and trees. This is the plan that transformed Xiakou. On the two-hour drive into the village, along a rising path from the provincial capital of Chengdu, John Flower pointed out the terraced and eroded cornfields in areas not yet subject to grain-to-green. The houses in Xiakou were surrounded by lush stands of bamboo and local softwood trees.

Families in the village now make their living from grain-to-green subsidies, by cutting bamboo and selling it to pulp mills, by part-time labor, and by the numerous small trades that characterize any Chinese town. The subsidies are scheduled to run out in 2016; by then, the farmers are supposed to have come up with other sources of income—so they don't immediately go back to clearing terraces and growing corn. One man we visited had formerly been a "rural butcher," slaughtering pigs for his neighbors and dressing the meat.

Government health authorities had cracked down on rural butchers. Now he drove a motorbike late each night into Chengdu, filled 50-gallon plastic tubs with restaurant waste, and drove the tottering load home to feed his own pigs. With the profits from selling two of their pigs, he and his wife had begun renovating their house and installing a toilet.

Although John Flower did not put it this way, as he talked with his contacts and reported their views, it sounded as if they were reflecting on the purposes of prosperity. By urban standards they were very poor, but looking after forests simply took less time than farming previously had. The main agent of local government, a village official in his thirties named Wu Wenlong, known as Long Long, whom Flower and Leonard had met when he was in his teens, told them about efforts to build the spirit and coherence of the village, so that young people would want to stay and enjoy a better-rounded life than was available as factory workers in the big cities, far from their families.

"In many ways this new project echoed previous policies of the socialist period and built on latent appreciation for the best of what socialism had given these people in earlier times," Flower and Leonard wrote in a paper about the attempt to revive Xiakou village. "One young man told us how much fun it had been when the first big distribution of [grain-to-green] seedlings came, for not since collective times had the fields been so filled with all the people of the village working together in a common task."

On a cool August evening in the mountains, Long Long had arranged for a traveling "courtyard projector" team to come in from the city and show Chinese movies against a big

239

white sheet hung outside a house. Two dozen families came from nearby houses to watch first a kung fu battle epic and then a movie about Chinese basketball. Long Long told Flower that it was a way to help them become a community, rather than letting each family sit at home watching TV. The national government had set the conditions for the shift in the village's economic base—but local officials were trying hard to shape the way the village responded.

YAOJI: DISLOCATION

Xiakou's people were trying to combine national policy with local initiative to make their village both economically and culturally viable. Neighboring areas were trying to survive the shattering effect of policy changes from Beijing and from the nearby county administrators.

The policy in question was, like grain-to-green, pro-environmental—in a sense. China's demand for electric power is voracious, and understandably so. Villagers who don't have lights at night want to have them, and then TVs. City dwellers want computers, and refrigerators, and air conditioners, like city people everywhere else. The main ways for China to generate more power are all bad: coal, oil, nuclear energy. It has the world's fastest-growing solar energy industry, plus big wind-turbine farms, but it needs more.

By comparison, hydroelectric power looks attractive. With its heavy rainfall, narrow valleys, and steeply descending rivers, Sichuan is a logical site to build hydropower dams. New ones are going up across the province—more than 350 generating plants are being put in along one river alone, the Dadu—and the low-lying flatlands along the river that their new lakes will submerge are where large numbers of farmers already live.

This means forced relocation—a national policy, but one that has been administered in quite different ways by county and city governments. In the village of Xiali, not far from Xiakou, Leonard and Flower showed us the results of a notoriously botched relocation. The largest dam project in Sichuan province dislocated more than 100,000 people when construction began in 2004. Some 50,000 farmers staged a protest in Hanyuan County, on land that would be flooded. They claimed that local officials were embezzling the money set aside for resettlement; according to Chinese newspaper reports, women cried when they saw the bleak new terrain that would be their future homes. Still they had to move.

Four years later, we saw some of these exiles. They were living in an area that resembled a factory yard, with long featureless concrete barracks partitioned into quarters for each family. As Flower and Leonard walked on a pathway between the buildings they asked families how they were doing and received a steady litany of complaints. The old land was fertile enough to handle several crops per year; the new land yielded only half as much. On the old land they had fruit trees; when they left, the compensation was a mere 20 RMB per tree, about $2.50. They were naturally not welcome among their new neighbors, since the new land that had been allotted was taken from someone else. Who was to blame? The farmers directed their wrath not at the national leaders who decided to build dams but at the local officials who, in their view, kept them in the dark about the plans, shortchanged them on compensation, and refused to listen to their complaints.

Perhaps because the social aftermath of the Hanyuan relocation was such a disaster, the next big Sichuan dam-building project was handled more deftly. We drove inland and uphill for several hours, until we reached an elevation above 10,000 feet, and confronted a scene whose scale recalled *Dr. Zhivago*. From one side of the horizon to the other, a recently completed dam spanned the Qingyi River. Behind it, a lake was slowly submerging the former village of Yaoji, famous for being the last stop on the Red Army's Long March before it crossed the snowy passes of Mount Jiajing.

The people of the village were mainly ethnic Tibetans, and they had been moved a few miles upland to a newly built city in Tibetan style. The windows, doors, and balconies had elaborate wooden fretwork, painted bright colors of yellow, green, red, and blue. The professional class—shopkeepers, teachers, police, government cadres—of the previous village were in a fancier village, with bigger rooms and wider streets; the farmers and laborers were in an economy-class version of the same structures across a ravine.

The fancy village had clearly been built as an attraction for Chinese tourists, a kind of Tibet-land. We asked innkeepers and merchants how things were going. Business had been slow since the earthquake, they said, but they assumed it would pick up in a few years. The guesthouse where we stayed was indeed busy when we were there, with guests from what appeared to be a convention of big-city policemen accompanied by flashy-looking and much younger women. (How did we know they were from the big city? Because they were so much bigger and heavier than the villagers we had seen over the past few days. In the Western world, the richest people are the trimmest, and the same is now true in China's glitzy cities. But in the hinterland, poor people are thin not because they're dieting but because they're short on food. The people who can afford to eat more, do.)

This relocation had gone better, because of more painstaking local attention—with one big exception. John Flower began asking villagers on the poor side of the new town whether they knew anything about Liang Heqing, a man who had lived in Xiaoji since the 1930s and who if he were still alive would be in his late eighties. As a teenager, Liang had traveled with the Red Army, for which his father was a guide. Recently he had been in bad health.

Flower asked, got no reply, and was about to give up—when, near the crest of the dam, he saw a pile of boards that looked like a demolished house and got out to look around. He pounded on a makeshift door—and after a few minutes it opened slightly and a face peered out. It was Liang and his wife, who over the next few hours told their own story of dislocation. It involved countless twists and strokes of bad luck, but its central theme was the family's absolute refusal to move off a final bit of their land that would not be flooded by the dam. The older members of the family remembered the Great Famine, and they thought that land would be their only security if hard times came again. "If they give us money, the money will go away," Liang said. "The only thing we can trust is land."

Apart from the simple drama of a Tibetan couple in their eighties hanging on in dire conditions, what struck me about the situation was the couple's faith that their cause, being just, would prevail. The law said they could not be moved without permission. (It was different for land that was being submerged.) Therefore they would stand on their rights. The villains, in their view, were corrupt local officials, in cahoots with the power company that was trying to evict them. Again, the role of "the state" was much more tangled than outsiders usually assume. National policy dictated a shift to hydropower; some local officials tried to arrange a relatively humane transition; others undercut those efforts.

BAOSHAN: ONE MAN'S INFLUENCE

We could not get near Wenchuan or Baoshan, the two cities with the largest casualty counts. The roads were still too bad, and still crowded with bulldozers and dump trucks. But evidence of the earthquake's effects was everywhere.

Before the earthquake, Dujiangyan was perhaps the most famous city in Sichuan, one of about 30 World Heritage sites in all of China. Some 2,000 years ago, an imperial official named Li Bing devised an irrigation system that would keep the Min River from overflowing its banks at floodtime and assure a steady flow to the fields the rest of the year. The stone irrigation structure is still in use and survived the earthquake. Many other structures in the town did not. The most notorious was the Juyuan Middle School on the east side of town. Its cement floors completely pancaked on top of one another, killing some 900 schoolchildren. Meanwhile the private school on one side of it, and the apartment building on the other, rode out the earthquake intact.

The field where the Juyuan School once stood is one of the few sites in Dujiangyan to have been entirely cleared of rubble. Elsewhere through town, ten weeks after the earthquake, buildings looked as they must have on the evening of May 12. Some were mere heaps of masonry; others had the roofs or windows shaken off; others had deep enough cracks in the walls or foundations to have become uninhabitable. The former inhabitants of those structures were on the outskirts of town, in makeshift tent-and-trailer cities that were already being prepared for long-term occupancy in the summer after the earthquake.

In the city of Baoshan, closer to the center of the quake, we saw a resort hotel that had collapsed when half a mountain slid down on top of it, and the remnants of a bluff, most of whose earth had been sheared off, buried cars and their drivers so deeply that they were never expected to be retrieved. At every intersection and on every wall hung big red inspirational banners: *Show the Red Army Spirit in Recovering from Hardship*; *Thanks to the People of Hainan for Their Help*; *Hearts Always Together*.

But we saw something more surprising in Baoshan. Half a mile from where the earth had shaken so violently that it dislodged the bluff, a modern building with a delicate glassy exterior stood shining with not a pane damaged. In front of it flew not just the bright red flag of the People's Republic of China but also two red flags of the Communist Party, with hammer and sickle in yellow, and another big Communist flag hanging in the front lobby.

This was the headquarters of the Baoshan Industrial Group, a modern company with a shared Communist ownership structure among most residents of the town. It had been led through its entire existence by a man named Jia Zhengfang, who demonstrated in the most forceful way the difference one local official could make.

Jia, now in his mid-seventies, came of age in Baoshan during the Great Famine. He saw in Baoshan that a sensible local official could blunt the effect of high-level idiocy by selectively ignoring the most damaging new rules. Where other villages lost half their population, Baoshan lost merely a third. Jia trained as a geologist, lost the sight in one eye in a mining accident, then came home to Baoshan in his late twenties to become a party official. He was beaten up by Red Guards during the Cultural Revolution but was popular enough to become a senior local party official by 1971.

From that point on, he helped his native village prosper by developing its collectively owned industry. He applied new farming tips to increase output. He developed lucrative mines for a variety of minerals. A paper factory and a small hydropower plant. A factory making wood flooring; a golf course; an eco-tourist resort; a Buddhist temple to attract tourists. The company published annual reports and had shareholder meetings, underneath the hammer and sickle flag. Based on his experience as a geologist, Jia knew that the land around Baoshan was unstable, and he made sure that the sleek corporate headquarters was designed to withstand a major quake. So were the villa-like houses built by the collective and available for townspeople. A study of Baoshan by two historians at Chengdu University said that it had become the "number one village in the mountains of the west" thanks to the leadership of Jia Zhengfang.

John Flower had requested an interview with Jia, and we went to see him inside the company headquarters. He was a jovial man, who stressed how the company had to keep looking for new business outlets. He said he had been dictatorial at times, but that was what the village needed. He then introduced his grandson, who he said was heading off for glory at Harvard. ("I am going to the University of South Carolina," he told us, in English, knowing that his grandfather would not understand.)

The same national rules applied in this village as in the others; the difference was local.

LUSHAN: COMPETENT GODS

Everywhere we traveled in Sichuan, Flower and Leonard kept an eye out for temples to revisit and photograph. She carried a GPS receiver to record the exact location of each site. (Chinese maps of the area are rare; the towns are too small to be identified by name on mapping sites or Google Earth.) He had a camera set up to take 360-degree panoramic pictures.

After a while, the pattern of the temples became clear. On the ground floor, most had shrines dedicated to Buddha, with scriptures and Buddha figures. Buddhism is one of the officially recognized faiths of China, and like the others that operate with state approval and under state supervision, it is considered no threat to political order.

But upstairs, or behind a curtain, or in a back room were other statues of other deities. These belonged to what Flower said was the "real" faith of China: They were local gods, folk gods, the god of wealth, the god of war, the kitchen god, at one shrine the chicken-footed god.

What these gods had in common was their practical utility. Each had a job and role. And a surprising number had been public officials. The powerful *chuanzhu,* or "river master" god, is based on the same Li Bing who built the irrigation system in Dujiangyan. A god-statue in one of the temples was wearing glasses; Flower said he was based on an early twentieth-century doctor named Lan who treated poor patients without a fee. It was as if Americans worshipped Alexander Hamilton or Benjamin Franklin—which perhaps they do, with likenesses on U.S. currency, rather than in religious shrines.

The government was skeptical of folk religions, Flower said, because unlike Buddhism or even state-controlled Christianity, they included an implied judgment on current affairs. People worshipped bureaucratic deities of the past when they were concerned about bureaucrats of the moment.

These were four small settlements, in one province, in one summertime week shortly while the area was recovering from devastation. It is nothing like a cross section of rural

Chinese experience, and I do not pretend to offer a full exploration of the range of local government performance. But even this limited range illustrates the point I mean most to convey: which is how varied the circumstances of this vast country are.

THEIR OWN WORST ENEMY

NOVEMBER 2008

After two years in China, there are still so many things I can't figure out. Is it really true, as is always rumored but never proved, that the Chinese military runs most of the pirate-DVD business—which would in turn explain why that business is so difficult to control? At what point in Chinese culture did it become mandatory for business and political leaders to dye away every gray hair, so that gatherings of powerful men in their fifties and up are seas of perfect pitch-black heads? How can corporations and government agencies invest huge sums producing annual reports and brochures and advertisements in English, yet manifestly never bother to ask a native English speaker whether they've made some howler-style mistake? Last year, a museum in Shanghai put on a highly publicized exhibit of photos from the Three Gorges Dam area. In front, elegant banners said in six-feet-high letters, *The Three Georges*. Why do Beijing taxi drivers almost never have maps—and almost always have their own crates or buckets filling the trunks of their cars when they pick up baggage-laden passengers at the airport? I could go on.

But here is by far the most important of these mysteries: How can official China possibly do such a clumsy and self-defeating job of presenting itself to the world? China, like any big, complex country, is a mixture of goods and bads. But I have rarely seen a governing and "communications" structure as consistent 'in hiding the good sides and highlighting the bad.

I come across examples every day, but let me start with a publicly reported event. Early this year, I came across a tantalizing piece of news about an unpublicized government plan in advance of the Beijing Olympics. In a conversation with someone involved in the preparations, I learned of a brilliant scheme to blunt potential foreign criticism during the Games. The Chinese government had drawn up a list of hotels, work spaces, Internet cafés, and other places where visiting journalists and dignitaries were most likely to use the Internet. At those places, and only there, normal "Great Firewall" restrictions would be removed during the Olympics. The idea, as I pointed out in "'The Connection Has Been Reset,'" was to make foreigners happier during their visit—and likelier to tell friends back home that, based on what they'd seen on their own computer screens, China was a much more open place than they had heard. This was subtle influence of the sort that would have made strategists from Sun Tzu onward proud.

The scheme displayed a sophisticated insight into outsiders' mentality and interests. It recognized that foreigners, especially reporters, like being able to poke around unsupervised, try harder to see anything they're told is out-of-bounds, and place extra weight on things they believe they have come found without guidance. By saying nothing at all about this plan, the government could let influential visitors "discover" how freely information was flowing in China, with all that that implied. In exchange, the government would give up absolutely nothing. If visiting dignitaries, athletes, and commentators searched for a Free Tibet site or found porn that is usually banned in China, what's the harm? They had seen worse of it back at home.

When the Olympics actually started, things did not go exactly according to plan. As soon as journalists began checking in at their Olympic hotels, they began complaining about all the Web sites they couldn't reach. Chinese officials replied woodenly that this was China, and established Chinese procedures must be obeyed. Were the arrogant foreigners somehow suggesting that they were too good to comply with China's sovereign laws? Unlike the brilliant advance scheme, all this was reported.

After huddling with officials from the International Olympic Committee, who had been touting China's commitment to free information flow during the Games, the Chinese government quietly reversed its stance. For a few days, controls seemed to have been lifted for Internet users in many parts of Beijing—in my apartment, far from the main Olympic areas, I could get to usually blocked sites, like any Blogspot blog, without using a Virtual Private Network, or VPN. Eventually the controls came back on, except for users in the special Olympic areas, and by then the Chinese government had turned a potential PR masterstroke into a fiasco. Now what the foreign visitors could tell friends back home was that they knew firsthand that China's Internet is indeed censored, that its government could casually break its promise of free information flow during the Games, and that foreign complaints could bully it back into line.

From the outside, this blunder might not seem noteworthy or surprising, given the dim image of the Chinese government generally conveyed in the Western press. It might not even be thought of as a blunder—rather, as a sign that the government had, for once, been caught trying to sneak out of its commitments and repress whatever it could.

To me it was puzzling because of its sheer stupidity: Did they think none of the 10,000 foreign reporters would notice? Did they think there was anything to gain?

The government's decision was more complicated but even more self-damaging in another celebrated Olympics case, this one the most blatantly Orwellian: the offer to open three areas for "authorized protests" during the Olympics—followed by the rejection of every single request to hold a demonstration and the arrest of several people who asked. It's true that even if China is wide-open in many ways, public demonstrations that might lead to organized political opposition are, in effect, taboo. But why guarantee international criticism by opening the zones in the first place? Who could have thought this was a good idea?

Such self-inflicted damage occurs routinely, without the pressure of the Olympics. Whenever a Chinese official or the state-run Xinhua News Agency puts out a release in English calling the Dalai Lama "a jackal clad in Buddhist monk's robes" or a man "with a human face and the heart of a beast," it only builds international sympathy for him and members of his "splittist clique." A special exhibit about Tibet in Beijing's Cultural Palace of Minorities this year illustrated the benefits of China's supervision by showing photos of grinning Tibetans opening refrigerators full of beer, and of new factories, including a cement plant outside Lhasa. Such basic material improvements are huge parts of the success story modern China has to tell. But the exhibit revealed total naïveté in dealing with the complaints about religious freedom made by the "Dalai clique." It was as if the government had hired *The Onion* as its imagery consultant.

Let's assume for the sake of argument that reporters are viewed with suspicion or loathing by the political or business leaders they cover. That doesn't keep governments in many countries from understanding the crass value of cultivating the press. Anyone with experience in neighboring South Korea, Taiwan, or Japan knows how skillful their business-governmental establishments are at mounting "charm offensives" to make influential foreigners feel cosseted and part of the team. Official China sometimes launches a successful charm offensive on visiting dignitaries. When it comes to dealing with foreign reporters—who after all will do much to shape the outside world's view of their country—Chinese spokesmen and spinners barely seem to try. I might be biased; my application for a journalist visa to China was turned down because of "uncertainty" about what I might be looking for in the country (I have been here on other kinds of visas). China's press policy seems similar to, say, Dick Cheney's—if without the purposeful stiff-arming—and reflects the same view: that scrutiny from the Western press is not really necessary. I'm convinced that usually these are blunders rather than calculated manipulation.

This is inept on China's part. Why do I consider it puzzling? Because of two additional facts I would not have guessed before coming to China: It's a better country than its leaders and spokesmen make it seem, and those same leaders look more impressive on their home territory.

Almost everything the outside world thinks is wrong with China is indeed a genuine problem. Perhaps not the most extreme allegations, of large-scale forced organ-harvesting and similar barbarities. But brutal extremes of wealth and poverty? Arbitrary and prolonged detentions for those who rock the boat? Dangerous working conditions? Factories that take shortcuts on health and safety standards? Me-first materialism and an absence of ethical values? All these are here. I've met people affected by every problem on the list, and more.

But China's reality includes more than its defects. Most people are far better off than they were 20 years ago, and they are generally optimistic about what life will hold 20 years from now. This summer's Pew Global Attitudes Project finding that 86 percent of the Chinese public was satisfied with the country's overall direction, the highest of all the countries surveyed, was not some enforced or robotic consensus. It rings true with most of what I've seen in cities and across most of the country's provinces and autonomous regions, something I wouldn't have guessed from afar.

Americans are used to the idea that a country's problems don't tell its entire story. When I lived in Japan, I had to reassure fearful travelers to America that not every street corner had a daily drive-by shooting and not every passing stranger would beat them up out of bigotry. When foreigners travel or study in America, they usually put the problems in perspective and come to see the offsetting virtues and strengths. For all the differences between modern China and America, most outsiders go through a similar process here: They see that China is a country with huge problems but also one with great strengths and openness.

It's authoritarian, sure—and you put yourself at great risk if you cross the government in the several areas it considers sacrosanct, from media control to "national security" in the broadest sense. (The closest I have come to trouble with the law was when I stopped to tie my shoe on Chang'An Boulevard, near Tiananmen Square in Beijing—and obliviously put my foot on what turned out to be a low pedestal around the main flagpole at Xinhua Gate, outside the headquarters of the country's ruling State Council. Three guards rushed at me and pushed me away to end this sacrilege.) But China is full of conflicting trends and impulses, every generalization about it is both true and false, and it is genuinely diverse in a way the Stalin-esque official line rarely conveys.

One other Olympics example: the Opening Ceremonies paid homage to China's harmonious embrace of its minority peoples with a giant national flag carried in by 56 children, each dressed in the native costume of one of China's recognized minority groups, including Tibetans, Mongolians, and

Uighurs. Contrary to initial assurances from Chinese officials, it turned out that every one of the children was from the
country's ethnic majority, Han Chinese. This was reminiscent
of Western practices of yesteryear, as when Al Jolson wore
blackface or the Swedish actor Warner Oland was cast as
Charlie Chan in 1930s films. But it was criticized by the
Western sensibilities of today.

Another element of the mystery is the deftness gap. Inside
the country, China's national leadership rarely seems as tin-
eared as it is when dealing with the outside world. National-
level democracy might come to China or it might not—ever.
No one can be sure. But from the national level down to villages, where local officials are now elected, the government
is by all reports becoming accountable in ways it wasn't
before. As farmers have struggled financially, a long-standing
agricultural tax has been removed. As migrant workers have
become an exploited underclass in big cities, *hukou* (residence-
permit) rules have been liberalized so that people can get medical care and send their children to school without having to
return to their "official" residence back in the countryside.
Whenever necessary, the government turns to repression, but
that's usually not the first response.

The system prides itself on learning about problems as they
arise and relieving social pressure before it erupts. In this regard
it learned a lesson earlier this year, when its reaction to the first
big natural disaster of 2008 turned into its own version of Hur-
ricane Katrina. Unusual blizzards in central and southern China
paralyzed roads and rail lines, and stranded millions of people
traveling home for the Chinese New Year holidays; the central

government seemed taken by surprise and was slow to respond. That didn't happen with the next disaster, three months later: when the Sichuan earthquake occurred, Premier Wen Jiabao was on an airplane to the stricken areas the same afternoon.

So I return to the puzzle: Why does a society that, like America, impresses most people who spend time here project such a poor image and scare people as much as it attracts them? Why do China's leaders, who survive partly by listening to their own people, develop such tin ears when dealing with the outside world? I don't pretend to have a solution. But here are some possible explanations, and some reasons why the situation matters to people other than the misunderstood Chinese.

There is no politer way to put the main problem than to call it ignorance. Most Americans are parochial, but (surprise!) most Chinese, and their leaders, are more so. American politicians may not be good at understanding foreign sensitivities and phrasing their arguments in ways likely to be effective around the world—as foreigners have mentioned once or twice in recent years. But collectively they understand that America is part of an ongoing, centuries-long, worldwide experiment and discussion about political systems and human values, and that making their case well matters.

After the 9/11 attacks, America went through a round of "Why do they hate us?" inquiry. Whether or not that brought the United States closer to understanding its problems in parts of the Islamic world, it represented a more serious effort to understand how the country was seen than anything I have heard of in China. When the Olympic torch relay this spring was plagued by boos and protests over Tibet in places ranging from France to the United States, the reaction at every level of the Chinese system seemed to be not just insult but genuine shock. Most Chinese people were familiar only with the idea that China has always been a generous elder brother to (often ungrateful) Tibet. By all evidence, no one in command anticipated or prepared for this ugly response. The same Pew survey that said most Chinese feel good about their country also found that they thought the rest of the world shared their view. That belief is touching, especially considering how much of China's history is marked by episodes of its feeling unloved and victimized. Unfortunately, that belief is also wrong. In many of the countries surveyed, China's popularity and reputation were low and falling. According to a report last year by Joshua Cooper Ramo of Kissinger Associates, most people in China considered their country very "trustworthy." Most people outside China thought the country was not trustworthy at all.

"The underlying problem is that very few people in China really understand how foreign opinion works, what the outside world reacts to and why," Sidney Rittenberg told me. Rittenberg is in a position to judge. He came to China with the U.S. Army in 1945 and spent 35 years here, including 16 in prison for suspected disloyalty to Chairman Mao. "Now very few people understand the importance of foreign opinion to China"—that is, the damage China does to itself by locking up those who apply for demonstration permits, or insisting on "jackal" talk.

During the Chinese Communist Party's rise to power and the civil war against Chiang Kai-shek's nationalists through the 1940s, the coterie around Mao knew how to spin the outside world, because they had to. One important goal was what Mao called "roping the whale": keeping the United States from intervening directly on Chiang's side. The future prime minister and foreign minister Zhou Enlai was especially skilled at handling foreigners. "He laid out battle plans and political strategies, in advance, with remarkable clarity," the muckraker Jack Anderson, who was a cub reporter in China, said of Zhou in his memoirs. "These truths made him so believable that a reporter would be inclined to accept his assurances, too, that the Chinese Communists weren't really Communists but just agrarian reformers."

Of course, most official voices of China now have the opposite effect. Their minor, provable lies—the sky is blue, no one wants to protest—inevitably build mistrust of larger claims that are closer to being true. And those are the claims the government most wants the world to listen to: that the country is moving forward and is less repressive and more open than official actions and explanations (or lack of them) make it seem. Many Chinese who have seen the world are very canny about it, and do have just the skills government spokesmen lack—for instance, understanding the root of foreign concerns, and addressing them not with special pleading ("This is China . . .") but on their own terms. Worldly Chinese demonstrate this every day in the businesses, universities, and nongovernmental institutions where they generally work. But the closer Chinese officials are to centers of political power, the less they know what they don't know about the world.

Even as the top leadership tries to expand its international exposure and experience, much of the country's daily reality is determined by mayors and governors and police. "It's like the local sheriff in the old days in South Carolina," said Sidney Rittenberg, who grew up there. "He'd say, 'They can talk and talk in Washington, but I'm the law down here.'" Thus one hypothesis for the embarrassment of the "authorized" protest sites during the Olympics: Hu Jintao's vice president and heir apparent, Xi Jinping, was officially in charge of all preparations for the Games. Hobnobbing with the International Olympic Committee, he would see the payoff to China of allowing some people to protest. But the application went to the local police, who had no interest in letting troublemakers congregate. A similar mix-up may well have led to the embarrassment over whether to open the Internet during the Olympics, and could also explain many of the other fumbles that get so much more attention than the news the government wants to give.

The Communist Party schools that train the country's leadership are constantly expanding their curricula to meet the needs of the times; but for advancement in party ranks, predictability, ideology, and loyalty are what matter most. The United States saw just how well a similar approach paid off in local and worldwide respect and effectiveness when it staffed its embassy in Baghdad's Green Zone mainly with people who followed the party line in Washington.

The frustrating consequences for China are obvious—though apparently not yet obvious enough to its leadership. For outsiders, the central problem is that a country that will inevitably have increasing and perhaps dominant influence on the world still has surprisingly little idea of how the world sees it. That, in turn, raises the possibility of blunders and unnecessary showdowns, and in general the predicament of a new world power stomping around, Gargantua-like, making onlookers tremble. The world has known this predicament before: It is what the previously established powers have feared about America, starting a hundred years ago and with periodic recurrences since then, most recently in March of 2003. Maybe that puts America in a good position to help China take this next step.

ALSO BY JAMES FALLOWS

BREAKING THE NEWS
How the Media Undermine American Democracy

Why do Americans mistrust the news media? It may be because shows like *The McLaughlin Group* reduce participating journalists to so many shouting heads. Or because, increasingly, the profession treats issues as complex as health-care reform and foreign policy as exercises in political gamesmanship. Or because muckrakers have given way to "buckrackers" who command huge fees lecturing to the very interest groups they are supposed to cover. Moving from rigorous analysis to concrete proposals, *Breaking the News* is a devastating critique that is indispensable for anyone who makes the news—and anyone who reads or watches it.

Current Affairs/Media/978-0-679-75856-3

BLIND INTO BAGHDAD
America's War in Iraq

In *Blind Into Baghdad*, Fallows takes us from the planning of the war through the struggles of reconstruction. With unparalleled access and incisive analysis, he shows us how many of the difficulties were anticipated by experts whom the administration ignored. Fallows examines how the war in Iraq undercut the larger "war on terror" and why Iraq still had no army two years after the invasion. In a sobering conclusion, he interviews soldiers, spies, and diplomats to imagine how a war in Iran might play out. This is an important and essential book to understand where and how the war went wrong, and what it means for America.

Current Affairs/978-0-307-27796-1

VINTAGE BOOKS
Available at your local bookstore, or visit
www.randomhouse.com